Too Smart for Her Own Good?

Too Smart for Her Own Good?

THE IMPACT OF SUCCESS ON THE INTIMATE LIVES OF WOMEN

by

Dr. Conalee Levine-Shneidman

and

Karen Levine

Doubleday & Company, Inc.
Garden City, New York
1985

Library of Congress Cataloging in Publication Data

Levine-Shneidman, Conalee.
Too smart for her own good?

1. Women—Psychology. 2. Success. 3. Intimacy
(Psychology) 4. Sex role. I. Levine, Karen. II. Title.
HQ1206.L47 1985   306.7   84-18803
ISBN 0-385-18820-X

For our families
Lee, Philip, and Jack
and
Alan and Noah

Acknowledgments

We would like to express our gratitude to the three hundred women who took time out of pressured schedules to meet with us and to talk openly about a subject they often found painful. We began writing this book with respect for these women, and our respect and admiration have grown during the process.

We would also like to thank Ellen Levine, our agent, for her continuing support and enthusiasm.

And we thank our editors, Kate Medina and Stephanie von Hirschberg, for their willingness to work with us, for their insight, and for their optimistic and sensitive support throughout.

Finally thank-you to J. Lee Shneidman and Alan Gelb for their ongoing interest and encouragement.

Karen Levine wishes to thank the Virginia Center for the Creative Arts for offering her a peaceful environment in which to make order of nearly three years of research, and to thank Helen Weingrod Levine and Isidore Levine for persuading her to enter the computer age.

Contents

Contents

The New Macho111
The Problem with Those Standards *113*
Developing New Standards Vs. Lowering Old Ones *114*
Pursuing the Intangible *115*
Recognizing a "Satisfying" Relationship *116*
A Closer Look at "The Perfect Couple" *118*
Looking for Trust and Goodwill *119*

CHAPTER 7
Farewell Fantasy, Hello Reality *121*

Looking for Real People *121*
Focusing on Accomplishment *122*
Focusing on Appearances *124*
Helaine and Adam—Good Man/Bad Husband *128*
Kate and George—Weighing the Priorities *132*
The Prize *137*
    Autonomy *137*
    Security *138*

CHAPTER 8
The Legacy of Female Sexuality *140*

Early Lessons on Sex *141*
Premarital Sex *144*
Conjugal Sex *146*
Owning Your Own Sexuality *150*
He Makes Me Feel Like a Natural Woman *150*
The Turn-On *153*
Women's Pursuit of Pleasure *156*
Seizing Control Vs. Letting It Go *157*
Noticing Sexuality *158*

Part IV
RELATIONSHIPS *161*

CHAPTER 9
Intimacy *163*

The Need for Adult Families *163*
Marriage: What It Was Supposed to Be and
    What It Was *165*

Too Smart for Her Own Good?

Part I

CAREER WOMEN: PUBLIC IMAGE VS. PERSONAL IDENTITY

CHAPTER 1

The Career-Woman Mystique

Heads I Lose, Tails You Win

Many successful career women today are frightened by their lack of success in forming enduring, intimate relationships with men. Many of these women assumed, when they embarked on ambitious careers, that fulfilling personal lives would somehow come hand in hand with achievements in the workplace. Work, after all, was the great challenge: It was what women hadn't done before. It seemed logical that any woman with the extraordinary talent to forge a successful career could do the ordinary as well—find a man with whom to share her life. But the equation, it turns out, is not that simple.

"I can't quite believe this has actually happened to me," said Arlene B., whose divorce two years ago coincided with her promotion to vice president of an investment-banking firm. "I'm two months away from my fortieth birthday and I make enough money to do pretty much anything I care to do. But I'm alone. The few men I do meet are either total losers or not marriage material. I live alone. I vacation alone. In fact, I'm beginning to see my future in terms of being alone. And it scares the hell out of me."

"Last week I went to my nephew's wedding," explained Janet K., a head buyer at one of New York's largest department stores, "and I realized that I was the 'maiden aunt.' When I got home and opened my mail I found a birth announcement from my college roommate. I had this overwhelming feeling of 'It's not *fair.*' I felt like the little kid who waits patiently while her friends pass around a bag of cookies, only to discover that by the time her turn comes there are none left. I mean, I'm a good person. I work hard. I look pretty good. I'm bright. I'm presentable. God knows, I dress well. I'm a nice person, damn it! So why do I keep coming up with an empty bag of cookies?"

The dilemma these women are experiencing is by no means unusual—it has become alarmingly commonplace. Significant numbers of successful career women have come to believe in a negative correlation of competence: The more competent they feel in the work world, the less competent they feel in their personal lives. *And they don't understand why.*

The ambitious, achieving career woman of today has hoped for more from life, on all fronts, than was available to generations of women before her. These women are in a very real sense pioneers: determined, energetic, courageous, and optimistic. In the past, most women thought they could have *only* love. Today's successful women want both love and meaningful work. They have struggled to establish a place for themselves in an unwelcoming, male-dominated work world, and their lives are, indeed, enriched by financial prosperity and the emotional gratification derived from a career. When they set career goals, however, few women thought they might be backing themselves into as restricting a corner as the one in which their mothers existed.

For more than a decade women have been intoxicated by

new options—heady, in fact, with the new experience of career responsibility, authority in the workplace, and economic success. Without realizing it, they bought into a career-woman mystique which presented itself as an antidote to the feminine mystique Betty Friedan wrote about in the sixties. Whereas the old feminine mystique promised a general sense of well-being and fulfillment to women who succeeded within its terms—as good wives and mothers—the message of this new career-woman mystique promised the same general sense of well-being and fulfillment to women who succeeded in the work world. It was, indeed, quite an alluring promise. Unfortunately, long-term, it hasn't panned out for many women.

Women caught in the new mystique didn't notice at first how one-sided their lives were becoming, but as they got older, their perspectives changed.

"When I was twenty-five," said Suzanne S., an attorney from Chicago, "I thought I had all the time in the world for everything. Now I'm thirty-five with no relationship in sight, and the ticking of my biological clock keeps me awake at night."

"When I moved into my first solo apartment I was twenty-two," said Judy A., an art director with a large West Coast advertising firm, "and I felt a real sense of independence . . . as though I were about to embark on a great adventure. Now I'm forty-two and still living alone. The apartment is bigger and more luxurious and the truth is I hate being there. It's the place I feel my 'aloneness' most acutely. So I keep a very busy schedule and come home only to sleep."

"I've been living alone for nineteen years," says Marie P., a retail businesswoman. "There's nothing I want more in the world than a committed relationship, but at this point I don't know that I'd be able to adjust to living with another person. I'm so set in my ways it scares me."

Money, which many women reasonably equated with "options" and "self-determination," seems less focal once it's been acquired. It *is* important, but clearly not an end in and of itself. With the passage of time and accrued experience, the rewards of the work arena have shown their limitations. Successful career women now dread the prospect of life without an ongoing, nurturing relationship. Consider the experience of Sandra T.

"Fourteen years ago," she explains, "when I got out of Radcliffe, a close friend and I met for dinner and we spent the night talking about our career goals. She was going into architecture, and I was pursuing, with every ounce of my passion, a career as a stage director. It was the early years of the Women's Movement and we felt we could do anything. We were smart, and hardworking, and obviously, high achievers.

"Five years later my friend had her degree and I, disillusioned with the sacrifices I had made to the theater, had decided to move into TV, where I thought I could use my brains and make some money at the same time. Seven years passed and we were still meeting for dinners and talking about our goals. By then I was a network executive in line for vice president. She was heading up her own firm. Within a few years, we knew, we would have both reached the goals we had talked about.

"For the first time, though, we began expressing this business of 'Are we doing the right thing?' Neither of us had any significant personal life. We both dated, but there was always something awkward about those dates. It was as though we didn't know how to play the game of meeting men."

This "game" of meeting men is something career women talk, and think, about a great deal. Their choice of the "game" metaphor is significant. These women are, after all, good game players. "Just explain the rules to us," women like Sandra seem to be saying over and over again, "and we'll study and practice until we learn how to win."

Games are manageable, particularly for achievement-oriented people. The rules for a successful career are very clear.

Too Smart for Her Own Good?

If one is smart, goes to the right school, or starts wi[t]
company, or finds the right mentor and works wit[h]
nation and dedication, one will succeed. Successf[ul]
understood those rules and adhered to them wi[..] dogged
dedication.

The problem is that finding a genuinely satisfying intimate
relationship cannot be reduced to a game plan, even by a
master game strategist. Women may succeed in devising
games that enable them to *meet* men, but rarely do those
games turn up the *kind* of men they need emotionally. This is
enormously frustrating for a woman like Sandra—for good
reason. First, she is accustomed to winning: to being at the
top of her class. And second, she is developing an acute
awareness of how much she wants the prize. Sandra knows
that she needs a relationship. People who lead extremely
pressured work lives—the very same people who often pro-
test that they don't have time for a relationship—probably
have the greatest need for the safe harbor an intimate, nurturing relationship provides.

"Here I am," Sandra continues. "A great success. And so is
my friend. Clearly we've arrived. But we both feel a bit like
casualties. It's almost as though we're handicapped in our
relationships with men because of our careers."

At this point Sandra's eyes well up and she takes a deep
breath, regaining control. She is feeling the negative correlation of competence we mentioned earlier: The better I am at
work, the worse I am with intimacy. "Why can't I get it
together with a guy?" she asks. "Why can't I do as well with
men as I do at work? I hate feeling like I can't do something.
I'm frustrated. I don't really feel desperate," she says, her
voice taking on a tone of desperation, "but I do feel sad . . .
and kind of bitter. And worried about my future in a way I
never anticipated. I feel on the one hand that I made a bad
choice when I committed myself to a career; but I know that
the other choice—being a wife and mother—would have

been even worse. It's like that joke: Heads I lose, tails you win."

The bitterness to which Sandra alludes is similar to the bitterness many women experienced when they felt those first glimmers of disillusionment with the feminine mystique —when they first acknowledged to themselves that their jobs within the home weren't enough. For a great many career women, however, that anger and frustration is compounded by the fear deep down that they have run out of options. Hence, the desperation.

Why are so many accomplished career women having difficulty establishing fulfilling personal lives? Until women begin to explore that question and its profound implications they will not be able to enjoy the full range of experiences to which they now, for the first time in history, have access.

The purpose of this book is to help women—married and unmarried—in that exploration, by examining how their career success, with all its rewards—financial independence, stronger self-images, etc.—has affected their ability to have intimate relationships.

To trace the origins of career women's feelings about men, work, and intimacy, we must go back to the time when those feelings were first formed: childhood.

The Lessons of Our Childhoods— What Mother Told Us

Most successful career women are not living the adult lives for which their childhoods prepared them. Most of the same women who are financially self-sufficient today were brought up, in fact, to be economically dependent on men. And they were brought up that way for good reasons. First of all, in the past men had access to money-making jobs; women didn't. Secondly, birth control had not yet reached the level of effectiveness we know today, and a woman expected to have children if she got married. She therefore had to be able to count on economic support during her childbearing years and beyond.

The impact of women's economic dependency was profound. It affected the way women went about living their lives, the way they felt about men, and the way they felt about themselves. The fact that women relied on men for money meant that they relied on men for all of the things money symbolized: status, authority, and, ultimately, even identity. And implicit in women's reliance on men for all of those things was their acceptance of a deferential position in their intimate relationships. Consciously, or unconsciously, they knew on which side their bread was buttered. They may have acted as though they were independent. They may even have believed they were independent. But the bottom line indicated otherwise. Women were locked into a system of economic dependency and the truth is that they were only as independent as the confines of that system allowed.

Good Husband/Good Wife—
The Old Ethos of Female Success

As long as women remained economically dependent on men they had to rely on the goodwill and continuing affections of their husbands. This reliance set the tone of their relationships. Women understood intuitively that an egalitarian relationship was not possible as long as they had no means of supporting the standard of living that they wanted and to which they were accustomed. Rather than pursue the unattainable, they dedicated their energies to getting what they could. Thus, the ethos of female success involved making a "good marriage."

Much of what a girl learned about relationships with men focused on how she could find the "right kind of husband" (translation: attract a good provider) and how she could be the "right kind of wife" (translation: optimize her husband's earning power and insure his continued goodwill). These two tasks comprised the "appropriate" lifework of women as it was laid out in the past. It was the way women had to take care of themselves.

A "good husband," a "good catch," or "marriage material," according to the lessons of our childhoods, was a man who was ambitious, hardworking, strong-willed, and successful. It didn't hurt for him to be strong-bodied, tall, and handsome as well. To the extent that a woman could find such a man, she was considered a success herself. To the extent that she didn't, she wasn't. Finding *a* man was not quite enough. A woman who cared about projecting a successful image had to find the "right kind of man." This message was powerful and, as we'll see, has been enduring.

The way to be a "good wife"—according to the lessons of our childhoods—made a similarly indelible impression on our collective unconscious. Women were good wives when they made their husbands feel powerful. It was women's job to bolster men's egos . . . to make men feel like kings in their own homes. The unspoken message was that women who were married to men who felt like kings would feel like queens. The hope was that if a man felt important and powerful at home, those feelings would carry over into the workplace. If that meant a woman had to tell men they were right, even when they were wrong, women did it. If that meant accepting, from their husbands, behavior they would not accept from anyone else, they did it. If that meant suppressing one's own ambition and growth, women did it.

Sometimes women did these things consciously. Sometimes they did them without even being aware of what they were doing. The anger that necessarily accompanied this deference was somewhat—but not entirely—mitigated by the feeling that one was succeeding as a "wife." By the standards of childhood these women were successful; and they experienced the gratification that accompanies any success.

In 1840 Alexis de Tocqueville (in his book *Democracy in America, Part the Second, The Social Influence of Democracy),* analyzed marriage in America as follows:

> In America the independence of woman is irrecoverably lost in the bounds of matrimony . . . The Americans require much abnegation on the part of women, and a constant sacrifice of her pleasures to her duties . . . Nor have the Americans ever supposed that one consequence of democratic principles is the subversion of marital power, or the confusion of the natural authorities in families. They hold that every association must have a head in order to accomplish its object, and that the natural head of the conjugal association is man. They do not therefore deny him the right of directing his partner; and they maintain, that in the smaller association of husband and wife, as well as in the great social community, the object of democracy is to regulate and legalize the powers which are necessary, not to subvert all power. This opinion is not peculiar to one sex, and contested by the other; I never observed that the women of America consider conjugal authority as a fortunate usurpation of their rights, nor that they thought themselves degraded by submitting to it. It appeared to me, on the contrary, that they attach a sort of pride to the voluntary surrender of their own will, and make it their boast to bend themselves to the yoke, not to shake it off.

De Tocqueville's observations held true from 1840 until the onset of the Women's Movement—when women began to struggle, with men and with themselves, to become autonomous adults. For a woman to become an autonomous adult, however, it is essential that she weed out the fundamental attitudes, values, and behavior (what we will call the AVBs) that she learned as a child and forge a new system of attitudes, values, and behavior to match her adult ambitions and strivings. This weeding-out process is difficult, particularly when it involves what we absorbed on an unconscious level as children. It is one thing for a woman to pay her own way when she's dating; it's quite another for her to have no inner conflicts about doing so—to not feel, on some deep level, that the man should be paying for her. It's one thing for a woman to recognize her desire for a nurturing, egalitarian relationship; it's quite another for her to feel sexually attracted to men who are genuinely uninterested in power and control. The old ethos of female success still exists, buried in the unconscious of many of today's achievement-oriented women. As a result, they carry around with them a set of aspirations and expectations about men that prevents them from developing more fulfilling personal lives.

Childhood attitudes, values, and behavior (AVBs) are, for the most part, absorbed unconsciously during the first decade of life, and from every imaginable source—parents, grandparents, friends, schools, TV, religion, literature, music . . . the backs of cereal boxes. Likewise, our response to them is unconscious. According to psychologist Benjamin S. Bloom of the University of Chicago, by the age of five most children have learned the general pattern of cultural mores and their parents' criteria for approval and disapproval. These early childhood lessons were, of course, very different for boys than they were for girls, particularly with regard to the relationships they would one day have with each other.

Looking for Men to "Look Up To"

Today's successful career women are still attempting to do the "appropriate" lifework they learned as children—the lifework of which de Tocqueville wrote. Although ostensibly women are no longer reliant on men for authority, for status, or for identity, they continue to relate to men in their personal lives as though they were. Their reliance, however, is camouflaged—even to themselves—by the accoutrements of their career success. Rather than acknowledge that they are looking for a man who will have access to power and take care of them, they express their reliance by looking for men whose accomplishments exceed their own.

Despite the fact that their public personas appear to be very different from those of their mothers and grandmothers, women who are financially self-sufficient continue to look for men to whom they can defer . . . men who can top them in a hierarchical relationship.

"I'm a partner in my law firm," said Ellen S. "I couldn't possibly become involved with a man who was still an associate somewhere." "I earn $75,000 a year," said Suzanne B., a Harvard MBA. "I couldn't imagine being in a relationship with a man who didn't earn at least as much as I do . . . or more." Women who have attained "x" are looking for men who have attained "x" plus. Their definition of the "right kind of husband" has shifted from "a man who will be a good provider" to "a man who will be a *better* provider than I am." The men they describe as attractive are, invariably, more successful than they are. The men with whom they feel sexual are more successful than they are. They grew up believing that husbands should be smarter, taller, more ambitious, more successful, and more powerful than their wives, and they are still looking for husbands to fit that bill.

And, of course, they often end up empty-handed. "There are no men out there," these women conclude. What women really mean when they say "There are no men out there" is that there are no men out there who earn as much as or more money than they do; or there are no men out there who carry as much status as they do; or there are no men out there who are as aggressive in their work as they are; and so on. They harbor the uncomfortable suspicion that they may have "priced" themselves out of the market. To be sure, when a woman earns $150,000 a year and will only be involved with a man whose earning power matches her own, she'll have a limited field from which to choose.

More significant, however, than the "statistical" problems career women face as they continue to pursue relationships that are governed by the hierarchical system of an earlier generation is what happens to those women when they succeed in their pursuit. What happens to women who are "lucky" enough to find the supermen they believe they need?

Getting It All and Having Nothing

The truth is that even when women find men who are smarter, taller, more successful, richer, and stronger than they are, they are not comfortable in the relationships that ensue. They lose even when they win. Achieving women are discovering that the natural consequence of finding the man whose achievements exceed theirs is the feeling of being overshadowed. For example, when women find these men who are more successful than they are, women feel *less* successful than they really are. When they find men who are smarter than they are, women feel *less* smart than they really are. Women who have spent the better part of their adult lives working hard to establish their own statuses and identities cannot feel loved—on an emotional level—when they are in hierarchical relationships premised on their deference . . . premised on their being relegated to the "lesser" position in a hierarchy.

Rarely do these women feel the sweet exhilaration of success when they finally find men who are smarter, richer, stronger, and more ambitious. Rarely do they feel the fulfillment that was the promise of their childhoods. Indeed, rarely do "winners" feel like winners for very long. What they do feel when they look for men—and when they find them—is a combination of anger, frustration, disappointment, fear, insecurity, and hopelessness.

Sometimes career women are aware of their feelings. Often they're not. Either way the feelings take a toll, both on the women themselves and on their ability to find gratification in an intimate relationship.

The ways in which these feelings show themselves and the ways in which they interfere with intimacy are manifold. Consider the following anecdotes, each of which represents a different point in the course of a relationship. For each we present dialogue just as we heard it, and then we present alternative dialogue. This is not a word game. The goal is not for you to memorize words that will make you a more successful social manipulator. Rather, it is to focus on the *feelings* behind your words. These are the feelings your words convey; and it is these feelings which need to be examined.

"If You Like Them They Don't Call Back"

"He didn't call me. I knew he wouldn't call," said Lynn K., a forty-year-old art historian, after she'd been on a blind date a few weeks earlier. "Want to know how I knew?" The question was clearly rhetorical. "Because I *liked* him. Rule number one of blind dates is 'If you like them they don't call back.' "

Lynn is angry and cynical with regard to men and relationships. What happened on that date? "Well," she began, "when we talked on the phone we agreed to meet for lunch. He's a tax lawyer and he works all the way downtown. I work uptown. He said he thought we should meet halfway and we agreed on a comfortable hamburger place in Greenwich Village. Then he began talking about how pressured he was with work and I suggested that I meet him closer to his office, but he said it wasn't necessary. When I got to the restaurant I looked around and picked him out. He was sitting at a table and appeared to be looking for someone he didn't know. I remember feeling very pleased when I saw him. I liked the way he looked. I walked over to where he was sitting and introduced myself. He asked how I knew it was him and I said, 'Well, you look like a tax lawyer. You're the only man here in a three-piece pin-striped suit.'

"We ordered and started talking. He immediately launched into a number about how little time he had, and I began to feel kind of annoyed. After all, I *had* made the offer to meet him closer to his office. Still, there was something about him that I liked. I was interested in him. He was attractive, successful, tall, and seemed like my type. I would have liked to see him again."

Height is a big issue for Lynn, as is physical appearance. She's a tall woman who spends a good deal of time and energy on her appearance. When we asked Lynn how she thought Tim, her date, felt about her initial remarks, she responded somewhat defensively. "What do you mean? I just told him how I picked him out. After all, he *was* the only guy there in a pin-striped suit. I think you're being kind of picky."

In fact, Lynn's opening remarks to the attractive stranger she was meeting for the first time were significant and may have had something to do with his not calling her for a second date. First of all, if Tim was, indeed, the only man in the restaurant dressed in a suit it's reasonable to assume that he might have felt self-conscious about his attire. Lynn's taking note of it the way she did couldn't have helped him to feel more comfortable.

Secondly, and more importantly, Lynn's first words to Tim told him what it was about him that she focused on. "You look like a tax lawyer," she said quite bluntly.

To be sure, one of the few things Lynn knew about Tim was what kind of work he did. He is, indeed, a tax lawyer and projects the appropriate image—something that his colleagues and clients all notice about him. But he associates those colleagues and clients with the pressures of his workaday world, and he's probably looking for a release from that in his personal life. More specifically, he wants to be with a woman who likes him and who can convey the fact that she likes him. Tim may not be aware of the fact that he wants those things, but he reacts to women based on his need for them.

Lynn, of course, noticed the things about Tim that made him "marriage material" according to her childhood system of values. They were, indeed, things she consciously looked for in a man. She had no problem saying "I want a man who is taller than I am, who's successful and sophisticated." The problem is that her opening remarks didn't convey the fact that she had been eager to meet him, that she was looking forward to their lunch. They had more to do with "taking stock" than they did with her emotions. If Lynn had been talking from her emotions the lunch might have gone differently. Lynn was, after all, eager to meet Tim. That was something she later realized that she might have conveyed on meeting him.

Consider the different direction Lynn's lunch might have taken if, when asked how she'd recognized him, she had said, "Well, you had a friendly voice when we talked on the phone and I looked around the restaurant for a friendly face to match it." Or she might have said, "I was a little nervous about being able to pick you out but you seemed to be looking for someone and you were, for some reason, very easy to approach."

If she had said either of those things—or something of a similar nature that she genuinely felt—she would have been connecting on an emotional level, which Tim might have picked up on. By not relating to him on an emotional level she was, in effect, denying her own emotional needs for human contact as well. She set the tone of the lunch based on the habits of her childhood AVBs, rather than attempting to examine the emotional needs she has as an adult.

When we asked Lynn to focus on her opening remarks she

became defensive and insisted that she had "acted very nicely." "I asked him questions about his work," she explained. "How long he'd been with his firm . . . what kind of cases he handles . . . the usual. I was really very nice." As Lynn described this conversation she appeared to be bored. The questions she asked were, to be sure, "nice." But "nice" is a bland word. Lynn's "niceness" bored her, and regardless of how good an actress Lynn is, it's likely that her boredom was conveyed. "Acting" is, by definition, not real. Emotions *are* real.

Lynn might have connected to what Tim was feeling—and to feelings of her own—by talking about pressure. Rather than ask Tim about his firm, she might have asked whether he liked his work enough to make all the pressure worthwhile. They might have talked about the way they each dealt with pressure . . . what they did to unwind. Or she might have talked about her own experience. "I haven't felt that kind of pressure since I finished my dissertation," she might have said. "I coped with it by eating. My best friend coped with it by *not* eating. I began to hate her. She got better-looking and I soothed myself with Sara Lee cheesecakes. It took me years to work them off."

If Lynn had responded to Tim in either of those ways, she would have had the good feelings that come when you offer friendliness. That good feeling would have been hers. "I'm a warm, friendly person," she might have felt. "How about Tim? Does Tim move toward me when I'm friendly or does he move away?" The answer to that question would have helped Lynn discover how open Tim was to a relationship. *That* is important!

The issue for Lynn on this blind date had to do with recognizing what she needs in a man and separating those needs from the things she grew up believing she needs. Her childhood focus is interfering with her adult needs. Until she learns to separate the two she won't feel that she can really be herself with men; and until she can "be herself" with men she won't get beyond the chitchat and cynicism. If you like them, and if you let them know it, it's more likely that they *will* call you.

Searching for the "Grown-Up" Man

Forty-year-old Sandy J. is the educational director of a private school in Washington. She's been married twice and lived with a third man for five years. She described her last date with a man she liked very much, and whom she had dated for four months, thus:

"The date started out just wonderfully. We went to a marvelous ballet and had dinner at an intimate restaurant. We talked a lot. He told me that his mother was beginning to bother him about grandchildren . . . and if she was ever going to have them. I know his mother through my own work and like her very much, and it wasn't unusual for us to talk about her. After dinner we went back to his place and I remember feeling very tenderly towards him. We got into bed and made love three times. It was marvelous. There we were, just lying together, when he asked me what it was like to be married and have only one person to make love to. 'What's it like to be married?' " Sandy repeated the question her friend had asked her, her voice taking on the tone of a six-year-old.

"I couldn't believe him," Sandy continued. "Jon is thirty-seven years old. For God sakes. He's a thirty-seven-year-old man! And he's never lived with anyone. I thought, my God, how could you get to be thirty-seven years old and not have even *tried* being committed to one person? I said, 'Haven't you ever lived with anybody?' I was incredulous. He said, 'no.' And he's so sweet, you know. And he's so good, and he's so good in bed, and we have such a good time when we go out. But I was astounded. I thought, what kind of a question is this for him to ask me? It sounded like the kind of questions the kids ask at school. I spend my professional life dealing with kids' questions, and I give them answers, so I tried to give him an answer too.

"I gave him some bit about how it could be hard, but also very fulfilling," Sandy explained, her voice beginning to take on the detached tone of an educator who's been teaching the same material for too many years. "After that night we spoke a few times but both of us were pretty busy and we haven't seen each other since. Part of me really misses him, but another part of me knows that it's better this way. He was a child. I'm not. I need a grown-up man."

In Sandy's case her anger—her contempt—was much more significant than any specific answer she gave to Jon. Why was Sandy so angry about Jon's question? The truth is that taken in its context—lying naked next to each other after having just made love—the question was a very tender one. In asking such a question Jon revealed his vulnerability. He *trusted* her with his vulnerability. In that trust there was a compliment to Sandy, but her anger prevented her from hearing it.

Jon said, essentially, "I am a thirty-seven-year-old man who appears to be a great success, but the truth is that I've been too frightened to live with someone." If Sandy had been able to recognize Jon's question as an expression of vulnerability —and if she had been able to accept a vulnerable man—she might also have recognized that Jon experienced his mother's desire for grandchildren as frightening as well. She might have said, "You mean you've never lived with someone," in a caring way, rather than an angry, judgmental way.

If Sandy had been able to accept this sort of vulnerability in a man she cared for, she might have talked about her own vulnerability. She might have asked Jon a question that genuinely reflected her concern without posing a threat to him. "Does the idea frighten you?" she might have asked. And Jon might have said, "I guess it must. I've never done it." Then

Sandy could have opened up a bit herself by acknowledging that "It can be frightening and lonely either way."

The night might have ended with a feeling of closeness, rather than distance—if Sandy had been able to accept Jon's vulnerability. She couldn't do that, however, without revealing her own fear . . . to Jon and to herself as well.

Although a part of Sandy is very drawn to a tender man, another part of her wants to be with what she calls a "grown-up" man. Translation: a man with as much or more experience as she has had; a man whose own vulnerabilities won't interfere with his ability to tend to her vulnerabilities. Unfortunately, the men who appear to meet these criteria are usually men who need to present themselves as invulnerable. And Sandy knows from past experience that she cannot build an enduring relationship with such men either.

New Women in Old Marriages

Arlene F.—an international banker—is married to Steve, an architect. Although Steve's professional reputation is outstanding, he doesn't earn nearly as much money as Arlene does. Her salary affords them most of the luxuries in their life and, despite an occasional twinge, Steve has continued to feel good enough about the work he's doing to have accepted that fact.

As winter approaches Arlene decides to buy herself a mink coat. Within a week of her decision she's had the first fitting, and less than a month later she's modeling the fur for her husband, who's not particularly interested at first, but is glad to see Arlene enjoy the fruits of her labor.

A week later Arlene visits her grandmother who is delighted with her granddaughter's coat. She looks at Arlene, smiles, and says how thrilled she is to see that Steve is doing so well.

"But, Grandma," Arlene explains, "Steve didn't buy it for

me. I bought it for myself. I've always wanted one. Isn't it spectacular?"

The grandmother's face drops. "He didn't buy it for you? You bought it for yourself?" She shakes her head. "I'm sorry," she says, her head moving from side to side. "It's not nice. You shouldn't have to do that. How can you enjoy a fur coat when you have to buy it for yourself? And," she adds, "think of how terrible you've made Steve feel."

Arlene is very smart. She launches into a diatribe with her grandmother about how hard she works and how she has a right to treat herself to luxuries that Steve may never be able to afford. Steve, she says, is delighted for her to have the coat. She leaves the old woman's home feeling annoyed. By the end of the evening, however, the anger has somehow shifted.

The next morning she doesn't wear the coat. Her pleasure has been tainted. That night she is very short-tempered with Steve. Over the course of the week she finds herself thinking things like "Why doesn't Steve ever work on weekends . . . like I do?" And "If he really loved me he'd find a way to buy me something luxurious. After all, those things are important to me." By the end of the week her head is aching and she is feeling generally uneasy.

Although Arlene, who bought herself something she had coveted for years, was sophisticated enough to appreciate that she and her grandmother lived very different lives, predicated on very different ideas of themselves as women, one comment from her grandmother had managed to put a substantial damper on her pleasure and threaten the harmony of her relationship with Steve. How could this have happened?

In truth, Arlene's grandmother simply embodied the voice of her granddaughter's childhood: a voice that measures a man's love for his wife by his ability to provide her with material things. Logic would have it that this equation is in need of adjustment, but logic does not rule the realm of feelings. Until Arlene is able to believe in her gut the diatribe to which she subjected her grandmother, her relationship with Steve will be precarious, and the extent to which she can enjoy her own success will be limited.

Fearing the Unambitious Man

Anne and her ex-husband are both social workers whose ambition has taken them beyond the usual limits of a social-work job. Anne has a thriving private practice, and her ex-husband, David, became head of a large social-welfare agency shortly before their separation. One of the issues that concerned Anne during her ten years of marriage was competition. "I never wanted to fall into a competitive thing with David," she explained. "I always made a great effort to support him in his ambitions. I always wanted to let him know that I wasn't threatened by his success. The truth is that I liked his success. I was really proud of what he accomplished, and I think he was proud of my work also."

Anne's efforts to support David's ambition and success were, to be sure, genuine. They do, however, have a historical precedent which often creates problems for women like Anne. It was the work of "good wives," as we said earlier, to tend to their husband's egos: to build them up and stimulate their sense of power. There's nothing inherently wrong with this "old" job; there is a problem, however, when it interferes with a couple's ability to communicate. Which is what happened with David and Anne.

"I remember the last summer we were together we rented a house in the Hamptons," Anne said. "It was the summer David was offered the top position in his agency, and he was not exactly feeling elated. In fact, he was feeling pretty depressed. One night we took a walk on the beach. It was one of those perfect summer nights. The moon was very bright. The sand was iridescent. We climbed up on a lifeguard stand and sat together looking out at the ocean. He began to talk about what was worrying him.

"I remember he said that he just didn't know if he was the man for the job," Anne went on. "He said he wasn't really sure that he was genuinely ambitious. That sometimes he felt that he was just caught up in some wave of ambition that was carrying him someplace he didn't want to go. He said he suspected that he was really a very laid-back man who liked wearing jeans and tee shirts and wouldn't mind spending the rest of his life in a staff position . . . dealing with patients. I had this reflex kind of reaction. I told him that of course he was ambitious. That he was creative and talented and that that was why he'd been offered the top job. There was no question that he could do it. He was too smart to stay where he was.

"While I was saying all of that to him I felt like I was being a good wife. I was giving him the same pep talk I'd given him throughout our marriage. I can remember hearing my mother give my father pep talks like that all my life. I really believed what I was saying. The thing is," Anne said very quietly, "that I realize now how unable I was to really listen to what David was saying. I couldn't even hear the feelings he was expressing . . . and those feelings were real and important. He really did question whether or not he wanted to move into an administrative position . . . whether or not he wanted to spend his days dealing with budgets and personnel. For some reason, and I'm not sure what it is, I just didn't want to hear what David was saying. And it's one of my great regrets."

One reason that Anne didn't hear what David was saying—that night or countless other times—was that she was trained, as a child, to respond to a husband's self-doubts with a pep talk. It was that training that elicited her response. Ironically, her professional training involved learning how to really listen for people's feelings, but when Anne is in the role of "wife," it is the earlier training that determines her response.

She responded to her husband the way she thought she was supposed to respond.

Another reason that Anne couldn't hear what David was really saying, however, was that Anne felt frightened by what she was hearing. Anne had no conflicts about her ambition. When she married David she needed to believe that his ambition met her own. When he suggested that perhaps it didn't, he was talking about changing the dynamics of their relationship. "I think," Anne concluded with great insight, "that I was more afraid of David's lack of ambition than he was. The idea of being married to a man who wasn't ambitious scared me. It scared me so much that I simply wouldn't hear of it."

Consider what might have happened if Anne had been able to just listen to David, if she had been able to hear him out. She might have been able to say, "What is it that you think you'll miss most about leaving the job you have now?" She might even have been able to say, "There's something scary to me about your passing this position up, but the most important thing is for you to be happy with your work. I'll have to figure out why I'm so scared."

How to Use This Book

The conflict between childhood values and adult aspirations is at the heart of the problem of many women's unfulfilled personal lives. Many women live with the conflict by slipping unaware from one system to the other—from adult behavior at work to childhood AVBs at home. Many of the women interviewed reported feeling "duplicitous" or even "schizophrenic." Still others expressed a generalized fear of being "found out." "I worry," one such woman explained, "that my husband is going to wake up one morning and discover that I'm not the gentle, loving woman he thinks I am. And I worry at work that my boss, or even the people who work under me, are going to discover that I really don't have what it takes for the job. Sometimes I feel like I'm involved in a charade that pervades every aspect of my life."

Of course, none of the women interviewed is involved in deception at work or at home. Neither are they duplicitous or schizophrenic. They are, however, caught up in a painful unconscious struggle to do right by two opposing value systems.

What successful women need to do is develop new AVBs, and thereby new, realistic expectations of men. This involves asking, and answering, the question: If I no longer need a man for financial security, or to give me status, or to give me an identity—if I can get all of those things on my own—then what do I need a man for?"

To answer that question you must first come to recognize the critical difference between saying, as many of the women interviewed said, "I need a man who loves his work and is as successful at it as I am at mine," and saying, "I need a man who will want me to share with him his pleasures, hopes, fears, frustrations, and disappointments, and who wants to share in mine."

This book is designed to help career women develop AVBs to fit their current lives—and form new, realistic expectations of men—through a three-step process. It's designed to make you more aware of your current attitudes and behavior toward men; and to help you adjust your outlook and behavior so as to improve your relationships with them.

In the ensuing chapters you will hear many different women speak about their relationships. The first step toward developing new AVBs is to listen carefully to what they say as well as to what they don't say—about their expectations from men; then try to ascertain what these women *really* need from men; and finally, try to identify the discrepancy between what they *say they need* and what they *really need*. That discrepancy represents the conflict between childhood AVBs and adult aspirations; and it is at the heart of the problem that successful women have with men. The insight that comes from learning to listen in this way is, in part, a resolution of the problem.

After you learn to recognize the signals of the clash between what was internalized as a child and what is needed as an adult, the second step involves turning your attention away from the women in this book and focusing it on your women friends. Begin listening to them with this newly developed barometer. Many of the women interviewed noted that "all of my friends have the same kinds of problems with men as I do." Indeed, many of the women interviewed spend a great deal of time commiserating with their women friends about their problems with men.

The thing to listen for is the extent your friends' expectations of men may be interfering with their chances of finding a man with whom they can build intimacy. What are their criteria for judging men? Do their criteria evolve from a system of AVBs that has become obsolete? Or do those criteria speak to what these women really need today as the mature, responsible adults they have become?

The third step requires that you turn your attention to yourself and to what *you* say when you talk about—and to—men. You need to question attitudes that feel as much a part of you as your own skin; to recognize where those attitudes came from and how they suit, or don't suit, your needs for intimacy today; and to consider what might be more fruitful alternatives. In the process you need to examine what it really means today to be a woman or a man.

"I don't have any illusions about finding the perfect man," said the head of a public relations agency who bemoaned the fact that there were "no men out there." "Well," we asked, "would you be interested in dating a bright, caring man who was a teacher?" "Sure," she answered. Then she paused and thought a moment before she qualified. "I mean . . . not a nursery school teacher, of course, but I'd have no problem with a college professor."

It is your job to ask, "And why can't he be a nursery school teacher?"—and evaluate the answer.

CHAPTER 2

Who Am I?—What Does It Mean to Be Feminine?

Identity—The Source of Inner Conflict

"When a society changes faster than the ideas of the people living in it," said Julia Kagan in a *Working Woman* survey on work in the 1980s and 1990s, "the pioneers on the cutting edge of those changes rarely have an easy time." Today, successful career women are just such pioneers, exploring the issue of gender identity. What does it mean to be a woman in the 1980s? What makes a woman attractive to men today? What makes men attractive to women? Today's independent working women are in the throes of grappling with these questions.

We said earlier that successful career women today are, for the most part, not living the adult lives for which they were raised and that the root of this difference involves economics. Women who were raised to be economically dependent upon men find themselves to be economically independent adults. And despite all of the obvious advantages of economic independence, on an emotional level that independence sparks a conflict with the attitudes, values, and behavior absorbed during childhood. Regardless of how successful women think they've been at rejecting those lessons of childhood that no longer make sense in their adult lives, the fact that so many of the career women we interviewed talked about "inner conflict" is an indication of how strong a hold their childhood AVBs continue to have on them.

Expressing the Conflict

It's no small task integrating the identity of a successful, independent woman with the traditional female identity most of today's career women were spoon-fed during their childhoods. The women we interviewed expressed their struggle in a variety of ways. Often, they focused on "little things," which seemed at first to be insignificant. They talked about these "little things," however, with a great deal of emotion. Clearly, they added up to something more important than they seemed at face value. When we focused on the issue of gender identity—on the definitions of "feminine" and "masculine" that each of us carries within ourselves— those "little things" began to make sense.

Stephanie G., a Chicago bank officer, exemplifies the struggle. "I spend the better part of every day supervising fifty men," she says. "I'm direct with them. I let them know what needs to be done and how I think they can best go about doing it. My attitude is that we all have a job to do together and any input towards that end is welcome. I'm not on a power trip. I'm just trying to do what has to be done as effectively as I can.

"I know for a fact that the guys I supervise like me, and that's important to me. They appreciate my directness. I feel really good about myself with regard to them. I feel like I'm most myself at the office. I'm very relaxed and confident. But when I meet a man socially I just don't feel like I'm standing on firm ground. There are lots of *little things* that make me uneasy. When I begin to enumerate them they sound ridiculous but when I lump them all together somehow they become powerful. They actually affect the way I feel about myself.

"For example, when I go out to dinner with a man and the waiter comes to take our order I find myself wondering whether I should order for myself or tell my date what I want and let *him* tell the waiter. If it were a business lunch I'd order whatever I wanted and assume that everyone else would do the same. Socially, though, I start thinking about whether or not my date will experience me as being overpowering. Words like 'unfeminine' and 'ball-buster' come to mind more often than I like to admit.

"After all, I don't want to be unfeminine. I want men to find me attractive. But I'm just naturally a very take-charge sort of person. It's fine and well to say 'just be yourself,' but if being myself means scaring nice guys off, it's a problem. On the one hand I feel like I don't want to be with a man who can't appreciate my strengths. On the other hand I don't want to be with a man who's going to let me run things in a relationship. Maybe what I think of as assets at work are liabilities outside of work."

What does it mean to be a "take-charge" sort of person? Clearly, on some level, Stephanie associates that quality—a quality that stands her in good stead professionally—with being "unfeminine." And the association troubles her both intellectually and emotionally. Intellectually she would like to believe that the old definitions of femininity and attractiveness no longer hold water. Emotionally, she suspects that they still do.

Betty H., the sales manager of a growing computer company, expressed a similar dilemma. "I can't seem to put it all together," she said. "I can get along great with men at the office—both the men I supervise and the men above me— but there just doesn't seem to be an easy carryover into my personal life. When I'm with a man socially I feel like Kate Millet and Marabel Morgan are doing battle inside of me. I want to be a sexy, gorgeous, irresistible woman, but I want to hold on to my self-respect and strength at the same time. I feel split down the middle."

Betty goes on to describe an incident involving one of the "little things" that troubles her social life.

"Until a few months ago I had always worn glasses. When I was sixteen I got contact lenses but they were uncomfortable and I basically gave up on them. But about three months ago I decided to give it another whirl . . . this time with soft contact lenses. The truth is that I look a lot better without my glasses on. I'm very much aware of that, but until recently I didn't really care enough to check out soft lenses.

"When I finally got to the ophthalmologist and tried the new lenses on I was delighted. They were more comfortable from the start than my old lenses had been after months of effort. So I began wearing them all the time. And I really felt great about the way I looked.

"Not too long after I began wearing them a man I had met at a party a few months before called me up and asked me out to dinner. I remembered having liked him and I was looking forward to the date. About halfway through the evening he looked at me and said, 'Weren't you wearing glasses when we met?' I said that I was, but that I'd just gotten lenses, and he started going on about how terrific I looked.

"The problem is that I found myself feeling very annoyed with this guy. All sorts of things went through my mind. I felt like asking him if I was so awful-looking when I wore glasses that it took him a month to call. Basically, I had a hard time really relaxing and enjoying the rest of the evening. When I got home, after he left, I realized that he was only verbalizing the very reason I'd gotten the contacts to start out with. It's true. I do look much better without the glasses. But the fact that it was a man saying so really irked me. And I'm sure he won't call again."

To be sure, Kate Millet, Marabel Morgan, Stephanie G., and Betty H. are all women. Their sexual *identity* is a simple matter of biology. Boys grow into men. Girls grow into women. But somehow Betty has come to regard being a "sexy, gorgeous, irresistible woman" as being incompatible with such qualities as strength and self-respect. She sheds her glasses in order to look more "attractive," and then feels annoyed by a man who makes mention of how attractive she looks without them.

Why does Betty feel that she has to make the choice to be either an ardent feminist like Kate Millet or an ardent anti-feminist like Marabel Morgan? It's no wonder that she feels "split down the middle." She has given herself too limitations; neither of which is a comfortable fit. Today's career women are, in effect, beginning to redefine what it means to be a woman. They are in the process of reshaping their images of "masculine" and "feminine"; and until they arrive at a comfortable resolution, they will continue to live in an uneasy state of flux.

Let's take a closer look at this process of reshaping gender identity.

Learning to Be Men and Women

"Who am I?" the career women we interviewed seemed to be asking. What does it mean to be *feminine?* What makes women attractive to men? What makes men attractive to women? On an intellectual level Stephanie and Betty both believe that they can be strong, confident, independent, and direct and attractive and feminine at the same time. On an emotional level, however, they're not quite sure. On an emotional level they seem to associate their strengths, their confidence, and their accomplishments with being unattractive and even threatening to men . . . with being unfeminine. It is this association that leads them to feel as though they're standing on unfirm ground when they're out with a man socially.

Their insecurity harks back to their childhoods when they first learned about how men and women *should* act.

What Are Little Girls Made Of?

Gender identity (or sex roles) is not a matter of biology. Rather, it is learned behavior that begins as soon as we notice our sexual identities. If sexual identity is the outer wrapping, gender identity is the filling. What does it mean, *inside,* to be a man or a woman? How do women act? What can women do? How do they feel? How do their feelings and actions differ from men's? How are they similar? Each of us begins to find answers to questions like these before we have the language to pose them.

The moment little boys understand that they will one day become men they begin to pattern their behavior after the men around them—specifically their fathers. And when little girls begin to recognize that they will mature into women they begin to pattern themselves after their mothers in much the same way—whether they ultimately admire their mothers or not. And mothers and fathers reinforce this patterning. The process is, for the most part, an unconscious one. Early unconscious patterning and years of reinforced role modeling combine to form our gender identities. It is this sort of early training that haunts women like Stephanie and Betty.

For the men and women who grew up before the Women's Movement—the same women who are in successful careers today—gender definitions were limiting and very specific. Men primarily realized themselves in the workplace. Women, whether they worked or not, realized themselves in the kinds of hierarchical relationships we discussed in Chapter 1.

"The traditional concept of the feminine role is one in

which the woman conceives of herself as the 'other,' " explains Dr. Anne Steinmann, a pioneer in the study of sex roles, in a collection of essays titled *Women in Therapy* (Brunner/Mazel, 1974). "She is the counterpart of the man and children in her life. She realizes herself indirectly by fostering *their* fulfillment. She performs a nurturing role."

Indeed, most of today's successful women grew up in a social environment that discouraged a woman's ambitious pursuit of a career. The discouragement was on two accounts. First, women who looked to work as a significant aspect of their identity were viewed as unfeminine and even selfish (i.e., "What kind of a mother/wife would leave her children/husband every day if she didn't absolutely have to?") Second, women were not considered to have the capabilities to succeed in the workplace. Women were fine within the confines of a relationship, but when they ventured out into the public domain they needed men to take care of them . . . to tell the waiters what they wanted to eat.

Both of those arguments are worthy of examination because they were a significant part of the environment of women's childhoods; and as such, they continue to impact on women today.

Career-Gal Image

The image of the career woman as being decidedly unfeminine was nowhere more evident than on the silver screen. There was Katharine Hepburn in *Woman of the Year.* There was Bette Davis in *June Bride.* And there was Rosalind Russell in *Take a Letter, Darling,* and all of the other films in which she portrayed the prototypical "career gal." Perhaps most insidious was Ginger Rogers's role in *Lady in the Dark* —a fabulously successful magazine publisher who enters into psychoanalysis so that she can chuck it all for the love of a domineering man who would otherwise be denied her.

The prototype required an attractive young woman to dress in a dark man-tailored suit with a severe high-collared shirt buttoned to her chin. Her hair was always pinned back in a tight, prim bun. She was punctilious. She was efficient. She was "brainy" and, invariably, myopic. She was competitive. Tough. Single-mindedly out to run the company.

As the plot progressed, we discovered that this "smart cookie" was, despite her denial, sexless and lonely. It is this image with which Stephanie associates when she thinks of herself as a "take-charge" kind of person. Clearly, it's not the sort of image one would aspire to.

What the "career gal" needed—and what she always found with the help of some Hollywood magic—was a man. Spencer Tracy. Fred MacMurray. Your average sort of fellow who would remove her eyeglasses and, somehow, give her a clearer view of the world. But more important for our purposes than this introduction of a sublime mate (which Betty, Stephanie, and most of the other women we interviewed would be delighted to welcome into their lives) is what the mate meant for the woman's career.

With rare exception, it meant the end . . . or a very significant wind down. After marrying the woman usually got pregnant, moved into a dreamy little cottage where she found *real* fulfillment—the kind of fulfillment she was always meant to have. The kind of fulfillment dictated by her childhood. The message couldn't have been more clear: Real women don't compete against men in the work world unless they're willing to do without men in their personal lives; men don't make passes at girls who wear glasses; any woman who's smart enough to do a man's job is too smart for her own good.

We have to stop and wonder how the actresses who played those roles felt about the characters they were portraying. Most of those actresses, after all, were earning more money from one film than the President of the United States earned in a year. Significantly, a great many of them also had very troubled personal lives.

Since today's career women were raised with the same message carried by such films, it's no wonder they feel conflict about their futures.

Gender Inferiority

In order to best realize one's role as the nurturing "other" in a relationship, women developed certain characteristics that were, later, equated with femininity. In order for men to realize their identities in the workplace they developed characteristics that were, later, identified with masculinity. These two sets of gender characteristics worked in conjunction with each other in a complementary, rather than a competitive, way. So, for example, if men were dominant, women were deferential. Dominance was valued in the workplace. Deference was valued within the confines of a traditional hierarchical relationship. Essentially, men were reared for the workplace—for the larger world and how to maneuver in it. Women were reared for relationships—for the smaller world of the home.

Dr. J. Rice, in an article in the *American Journal of Psychiatry,* listed some traditional male and female values as follows: It was considered masculine to be independent and feminine to be dependent; it was considered masculine to be active and feminine to be passive; it was considered masculine to be logical and feminine to be emotional; it was considered masculine to be strong and feminine to be fragile.

Most researchers in the field of gender identification observed the same things. "Women *are perceived* as relatively less competent, less independent, less objective, and less logical than men," reports Dr. I. K. Broverman in *The Journal of Social Issues.* "Men," she continues, "are perceived as lacking interpersonal sensitivity, warmth, and expressiveness in comparison to women. Moreover, stereotypically masculine traits are more often perceived to be desirable than are stereotypically feminine characteristics."

Most recent studies continue to demonstrate the existence of clearly defined sex-role stereotypes for men and women, despite life-styles that seem to indicate otherwise. The Women's Movement will have a significant effect on the way today's young children grow up experiencing femininity and masculinity because it changed the life-style of their parents; but that change in life-style doesn't necessarily represent a comparable emotional change. Women who are successful in the workplace today may, or may not, feel less competent than the men with whom they work; but however they've resolved that issue in the workplace doesn't appear to have necessarily carried over into their personal lives; neither with regard to their expectations of men nor their feelings about themselves.

When it comes to career women's personal interactions with men—interactions that take them out of the realm of the work world where they have managed to relate to men as peers and into the realm of relationships where they have been trained to act deferentially—many women continue to march to the drum of their childhood AVBs. Of course, relating to men one way at work and another way at home takes its toll. It creates inner conflict and confusion and leaves women feeling very much the way Betty H. does: "split down the middle," and not quite sure who she *really* is.

Dr. Steinmann observed this dilemma in the course of her research. "Women universally share a desire to combine self-realization with the more traditional nurturant roles bestowed on them in part by their biology," she reports, "and they share a perceived conflict between the activity and independence they would like, and the passivity and dependence men want them to exhibit. . . . There is a consistent conflict in women's minds as to what their role should be, a

feeling that in order to please men they will have to be
untrue to themselves."

Essentially, career women must grapple with two questions, one of which is the flip side of the other. First, "How
does a woman who has been 'bred' for relationships find
success in the workplace?" And second, "How does a woman
who has 'reoriented' herself for the workplace turn around
and find success in relationships?"

All of the women we interviewed have managed to answer
the first of these two questions for themselves. Saddled with
their (often unconscious) sense of gender inferiority they
moved into the work world to compete with men. They
found ways to overcome their "breeding"—to overcome the
sense of inferiority implicit in their earliest gender identification—and become successful at work. It was, as we'll see, no
small task.

It's our contention, however, that something about the
way women have gone about resolving this first question has
hindered their ability to resolve the second. Something about
the way today's successful career women coped with the
issue of their traditional gender identity in the workplace has
made it difficult for them to find satisfying personal relationships with men. Let's look at both parts of the problem more
closely.

How Women Bred for Relationships
Find Success at Careers

Women's traditional sexual stereotyping did more than
simply *fail to prepare* women for the workplace. In a much
more active sense, traditional sexual stereotyping *prepared
women to fail* in the workplace. As we noted earlier, women
entered the competitive world of work with a set of childhood AVBs that told them they were somehow "less than"
the men with whom they would be competing. Those old

AVBs were very clear about women competing against men: Men won and women lost.

Beyond that distinct handicap, however, was the fact that the world of work was defined by men. Men made the rules. Men set the tone. The issue of potential capabilities aside, boys learned from an early age the values of the workplace (i.e., logic-think, competitiveness, personal ambition, etc.) and, as a result of this early training, men had the cards stacked decidedly in their favor once they began working. Clearly, the easiest way to make it in a man's world was to enter it as a man.

All of the characteristics for which girls were rewarded—like passivity, vulnerability, and dependence—were experienced as burdens by women once they began to pursue ambitious careers; and with good reason. The fact was that traditional female assets *were* liabilities in the work world. The impulse to compete, for example, was more valuable than (and directly in conflict with) the impulse to support and nurture.

Smart, ambitious, determined women read the situation very well. "Women's greatest hurdle to overcome if they want to be successful," a woman on the board of three Fortune 500 companies says, "is the fact that they didn't grow up with male egos." She makes this statement in the most matter-of-fact way, and hundreds of women nod in eager agreement when we present her edict to them. In 1982, Korn/Ferry International published a *Profile of Women Senior Executives.* When Korn/Ferry asked, "What was the greatest obstacle you had to overcome to achieve your success?" nearly 40 percent of the women executives answered, "Being a woman."

When these women equated "being a woman" with "being a problem," they were not talking primarily about the issue of minority discrimination. In fact, only 8.8 percent of the women in the Korn/Ferry study pinpointed "convincing others of ability" as an obstacle to their success. Rather, they were talking about the problems of growing up passive rather than active; dependent instead of independent; emotional instead of logical, and so forth.

Carol J., a partner in a large public accounting firm, elaborates on the problem from her own experience. "When I say that being a woman was an obstacle to my success, I'm not just talking about what a hard time I had breaking into the old-boys' network. I'm talking, really, about breaking out of the old-girls' network. I've spent an enormous amount of energy in my career just keeping tabs on my female ego . . . just keeping the logic flowing instead of the emotions.

"For example, several years after I first began working here," Carol recalls, "I was involved in the audit of a big international conglomerate. It was a very complicated situation and I was doing very well with it. I really enjoyed the work. The problem was that the CEO of that company had a hard time accepting me as the on-site head of the project because he'd never dealt with a woman in that capacity before. It was clear to me that he wasn't very comfortable with women, and there wasn't a damn thing I could do about it. After a few weeks the senior partner in charge of the audit pulled me off.

"Needless to say I was in a rage. I felt that they had no right to do it. After all, it wasn't *my* problem. It was the problem of the CEO. I stomped around the office for a long time after that. I began feeling very insecure . . . as though I had been personally rejected. I worried about how it would reflect on me to have been taken off this major audit. And I worried about whether or not I was good enough . . . even though I knew, on some level, that I had done just fine.

"Of course, I was immediately put on another job, and there was no problem with it. But I was peeved. After a few weeks, the managing partner of our firm called me into his office and gave me what amounted to a lecture. He said that I'd have to get my act together. From the perspective of the firm, they needed to take care of major clients in ways that

kept them happy. That—and doing a good job—was what
they cared about. He could understand that it was a frustrating experience for me, but he felt I was personalizing the
whole thing instead of viewing it from a business perspective. That particular job was more likely to be done in a
satisfactory way by someone other than me.

"Obviously, since I did manage to become a partner here
several years ago, I was able to take myself in hand. When I
begin to feel very emotional about something at work, and
outside of work as well, I can stop now and put a check on the
emotions. Usually I'm able to move forward with a clear
head. Sometimes I stop and think about how one of the male
partners might react in a similar situation. That's helpful."

Carol and many other successful career women have managed to get over the "hurdle" of being women by patterning
themselves after men. Hollywood's depiction of the "career
gal" as a woman in man's clothing (both literally and emotionally speaking) was accurate. It was a simple matter of
"When in Rome . . ."

In order for women to achieve success for themselves they
had to see themselves fitting into a world men created.
Women who entered the workplace in search of serious careers didn't have other women on whom they could pattern
themselves. Reasonably, they patterned themselves after
men. Men held the positions to which they aspired.

Indeed, women had a great deal to learn from men about
the male-dominated work world. Carol's approach—"Sometimes I stop and think about how one of the male partners
might react in a similar situation"—made sense, but it often
comes with a price.

The problem is that it isn't always easy for women to shed
the "clothing" they wear at the office. Many of them find
when they shed their "office clothing" and go to the closet for
a new outfit that they have "nothing to wear."

Part II

THE CONSEQUENCES
OF ABSORBING
MALE CHARACTERISTICS

CHAPTER 3

Squeezing into a Male Image

The first problem women had to deal with when they began to pursue ambitious careers was, as we said earlier, how they could overcome a childhood that prepared them to fail in the work world. We've discussed the fact that many women overcame their "breeding" by squeezing themselves into a masculine image at work; and as long as women stayed within the work world they had no problem with their newly developed AVBs.

But how does one navigate between the world of work and the world of relationships? That is a problem with which men never had to deal. What was expected of a man in traditional relationships and what was expected of him in the workplace did not fuel a conflict. Indeed, traditional relationships were formulated in such a way as to offer men both emotional and practical support while they pursued ambitious careers.

In order for women to manage both a career and a relationship, however, they had to be "superwomen," not so much because the *physical* tasks were so overwhelming, but rather because the job of switching gears *emotionally* to suit their surroundings was nearly impossible. Still, women tried to meet the challenge. They wanted work and they wanted love, and they attempted—both consciously and unconsciously—to get both.

Of course, they ran into problems along the way. One reason they encountered such difficulty is that the process by which women squeezed into male images in the work world was often not a conscious one. They didn't always say to themselves, as Carol did, "How would a man act in this situation?" More often, they learned the AVBs of the men around them in much the way they learned female AVBs when they were children. It was the most natural thing in the world. They observed, imitated, and eventually internalized the attitudes, values, and behavior of the world to which they aspired. And as long as they stayed within that world they had no problem.

"I'm so comfortable at the office, and I do so well there," said Emily G., a vice president in charge of corporate communications for a large pharmaceutical company, "that I don't always feel like leaving. I sometimes find myself getting tense when Friday rolls around, though. I'm most comfortable when I feel productive. And I always feel productive at work. I know what's expected of me there. I wish I could say the same for my personal life."

Emily said she's comfortable at work because she knows what's expected of her there, and uncomfortable with men because she doesn't know what's expected of her with them.

"If I have a date," she noted, echoing many of the women we have already discussed, "I'm never sure of what's expected of me. I feel like there's some piece of myself missing when I'm not in a relationship, and I feel like there's something wrong with me when I *am* in one."

In fact Emily's discomfort with men has more to do with what she *thinks* they expect of her than with the possibility that those expectations are unknown. Deep inside, Emily still views relationships as hierarchical power systems in which men hold the power. If men hold the power, it is inevitable that women must be deferential . . . that Emily must be deferential. This is her unconscious belief. Consciously, however, Emily believes that she is equal to a man and she wants a relationship premised on that equality. Therein lies her conflict.

How do women like Emily resolve the conflict they feel when they leave the world of work and enter the world of relationships? Based on our interviews it appears that they resolve this incompatibility in one of two ways. Either they struggle, consciously and unconsciously, to maintain their work image (i.e., male identification) outside of the workplace as well as within, or they struggle to maintain a male identification while they are at work and a female identification when they leave the workplace.

Each option poses its own set of problems. Let's examine the two options, see how they are manifested, and then look at the problems inherent in each.

Work and Love: Creating an Artificial Consistency

The issue of "consistency" is critical to many career women. What they mean is that it's important to them that they be the same person during the workday as they are in their personal relationships outside work hours. They want to be "true to themselves." If they have internalized a set of male AVBs in the workplace, they expect those same AVBs to serve them in their personal lives as well, and it doesn't work that way.

"I am what I am," says Joanna K., a forty-year-old oil broker who has been married to the same man for ten years. Rick, her husband, is a lawyer. "I didn't put on any acts when I was dating Rick. He saw exactly what he was getting. He knows that my work is very important to me. He understands that I have to travel, and that I'm always under the gun. If he should decide at some point that he doesn't like that about me, the issue will be that he's changed his mind . . . not that I've been caught in a charade."

Joanna's statement sounds perfectly reasonable. It is, indeed, admirable to be "true to oneself." Joanna has found refuge from conflict in her consistency. She doesn't have to struggle, as many other women do, with the feeling that her work persona and her private persona clash.

Her resolution of the problem, however, is not all that neat. Joanna, and other women who have internalized the AVBs of the workplace, may succeed in escaping from one sort of conflict; but their escape often brings with it a different set of problems.

Denying the Value of Feelings

Joanna has what she herself calls a "reasonably good marriage. But," she adds, assessing her relationship with a good deal of thought and consideration, "it's not without problems. For example, a few weeks ago Rick started bemoaning the fact that he didn't make as much money as he should." (She earns more than $200,000 a year and her husband earns roughly half of that.)

"We were sitting in a restaurant having dinner when he first brought it up," she explains. Her voice conveys great fatigue. "I asked him how much he wanted to be earning and he said that there was no reason why he shouldn't be earning twice what he's making now. There are partners in his firm who pull in $200,000. And I agreed with him. Not only did I agree with him, but I set out to help him. I started exploring all the ways he could double his earning capacity. He could be tougher. God knows, he could be much more organized. He doesn't have the kind of follow-through that he might. And he's not aggressive enough about going after clients.

"Ever since that evening he's been totally inaccessible.

He's depressed. He's not interested in sitting and talking, let alone having sex. He's really closed himself up. I just can't handle coming home from work to this for much longer. It's too exhausting. I'm not his mother, after all. Rick knew very well that if he asked me for my opinion on something like this I'd give it to him . . . straight from the hip."

Joanna spends her days in a pressured environment making deals. She uses logic, persistence, and intelligence. She's tough and very competitive. All of these qualities—which are the traditional male AVBs we discussed earlier—contribute to her extraordinary success. They don't, however, work the same way in the context of her marriage. Tenderness and nurturing are more important in an intimate relationship than are the skills Joanna uses all day long trading oil. She has to listen with a different kind of ear in an intimate relationship than the one she uses at the office. Yet Joanna clearly feels disdain for those relationship skills, which she regards as the sort of thing a "mother" would do. For her, the word "mother" connotes a softness more akin to weakness than to emotional strength.

Indeed, many women who have attempted to reject their childhood AVBs have come to think of "mothering" in a negative way. Unfortunately, women like Joanna have come to regard the sensitivity and wide range of feelings to which women have access as being, somehow, a betrayal of the AVBs they adopted as adults. When they experience feelings that are rooted in their childhood AVBs—when they feel the impulse to be nurturing and tender, for example—they often feel they are being "duplicitous," "hypocritical," or, as in the case of Joanna, "weak" and "insincere."

Much of what women learned as children about nurturing, softness, and sensitivity was taught in the context of a system that assumed women's intrinsic helplessness; a context that assumed women needed men to care for them. Women who are no longer helpless need not abandon their nurturing, soft, and tender qualities, however. These same qualities can be the foundation for a mature, humanistic system of values, and signs of strength rather than weakness. Women like Joanna unconsciously have taken what might be considered a great strength—their access to a wider range of feelings than most men have—and turned it into a flaw.

Imagine that Joanna had made more of an effort to ferret out Rick's problem when he began "moaning," rather than tackling it. Clearly, his earnings—which are high by most standards—are adequate, when combined with hers, to support an unusually luxurious life-style. Joanna recognizes, when she says that she's not Rick's mother, that his *feelings*—not their bank account—are in need of attention. Why not address them? The message that says feelings—particularly feelings of inadequacy—are not worthy of attention and care comes from the male AVBs Joanna has internalized for the workplace.

"I just can't be a nursemaid to his ego," she answers defensively. Somehow, Rick's feelings of inadequacy have become, in Joanna's mind, an expression of such grave weakness that they require not only the care of a mother, but the care of a nurse as well. "The fact," she adds, "is that Rick was right in his evaluation. He *should* earn more money than he does. And it would have been phony of me to lie about it or tell him he's terrific at something when, in fact, I know he could be much, much better. My integrity is worth something here too. After all, when Rick and I got married he knew I wasn't the kind of *little* woman who would spend all my time telling him how big and strong he was. I was only telling him the truth. What's wrong with that?"

Joanna cannot change gears emotionally when she leaves the workplace without feeling that she's being duplicitous—without feeling that the *kind* of woman she worked so hard to become will be threatened by the *kind* of woman she struggled to avoid being—her mother. Although she didn't sacrifice being in a relationship, she *did* sacrifice being tender and nurturing in a relationship when she made a decision to be "exactly the same at work as I am at home." And she punishes herself by using the word "duplicitous" when she feels the impulse to address her husband's feelings.

Joanna opted for toughness, and professionally her choice panned out. But she's unable to change her mode of response when she leaves the office and enters into the sphere of intimacy a relationship encompasses. She has turned down a one-way street and can't find a way out. When she absorbed the AVBs of the workplace, she felt the need to abandon, forever, the traditional female AVBs that might have helped her in her relationship with Rick. Those qualities were all right for her mother—or for Rick's—but they don't cut the mustard in the world she's chosen. She can't afford to be like her mother to any degree because she believes that doing so will threaten the professional success that's been a decade in the building.

Career women who choose to carry their work AVBs over into their personal lives are often protective of their independence and strength in much the way children of the Depression came to be protective of their financial security. In both cases there is a great concern—understandable concern—about losing something that was hard won. On some level, children of the Depression never quite believe that they don't have to worry about money, and women who have just moved up in caste and class don't quite believe that their accomplishments are anything but tenuous. All of the attributes of traditional female AVBs represent, for Joanna, a return to the old pattern of domesticity—a return to the kind of dependent relationships she worked so hard to avoid. Those attributes frighten her more than she knows. Her fear of them, however, has led her to throw out the baby with the bathwater. And if her marriage breaks up she will say that it was because her husband was too weak, or too threatened by her, or too competitive. She will not understand the extent to which her fear of her own tenderness was responsible.

Of course, if Joanna hadn't been led down a one-way street

that offered no opportunity for warmth and nurturing, she
might have been able to open herself up to a wider range of
emotional responses; in which case the conflict would not
have existed. She wouldn't have had to feel that she was
betraying her very self if she looked to her mother (or looked
to traditional female AVBs) for a way of dealing with a particular problem. Many women share Joanna's feeling of duplic-
ity when they act significantly different in the workplace
than they do in their private lives.

Let's consider some other ways the same problem ex-
presses itself.

The Aggressive Mentor

Until very recently career women have, necessarily,
looked to men as mentors. For one thing, there just weren't
many women in high places. For another, those few women
who *had* made it to the top were often unavailable, unattractive role models cut in the Hollywood image we discussed
earlier. A recent New York *Times* article, in which many
successful women were interviewed, concluded that in large
part these women attributed their success to a man . . . a
mentor.

The Greek ideal of a mentor, as a wise and trusted coun-
selor, is very appealing. But as a result of all the years during
which men actively (although not always individually) ex-
cluded women from positions of power, the dynamic between women at work and the men they looked up to has
become much more complex than that of mentor-devotee.
By and large, men have, historically, been committed to
keeping women down. How have they suddenly been elevated to the position of mentor . . . with all the trust implicit in that role? Surely history has given women no basis
for this trust; for it was history that shaped the childhood

system of values of most men from whom women seek advice.

Are there exceptions? Most likely. But significant numbers of career women are willing to swallow whole the advice of their mentors . . . regardless of how ill-advised or ill-intentioned it may be. One reason these women are so willing to accept what we consider to be damaging advice from men is that they, themselves, have incorporated the AVBs of the men with whom they identify. They cannot afford—emotionally—to question these AVBs.

Women can, of course, learn a great deal from men, particularly with regard to the work world. To be sure, there are many men who offer genuine, heartfelt advice. In no way do we suggest that all men are malevolently plotting the return of women to *Kinder, Küche,* and *Kirche.* Yet it is uncharacteristically naive of career women *not* to look beyond the most apparent level of what men offer in the way of advice.

Consider the following experience. Sara, a thirty-eight-year-old woman, was recently made a partner in a Chicago law firm. She recollected a conversation which, in retrospect, she identified as "pivotal" between herself and a senior partner in the firm. At the time of the conversation Sara was an associate, being considered for partner, and the senior partner was a man she proudly identified as her mentor.

"He came into my office," she said, "just prior to the time I came up for partner and said, point-blank, that he thought I was a brilliant lawyer with a terrific future in the firm, but that I had some very critical decisions to make. And he said that it was only because he cared for me on a personal level that he was even addressing me on this level, but he wanted me to understand that the hard work—the late hours and weekends—didn't end when someone became a partner. In a sense . . . a very real sense . . . the responsibilities increased. Basically, he said that he knew I had sacrificed a lot on the personal front while I worked as an associate, and that

I'd probably be called upon to continue making the same sacrifice. He warned me that it would be hard to find a man who'd be really sympathetic to the kind of schedule I'd have to keep . . . and he went so far as to admit that *he* personally could never be married to such a woman. He needed someone who, like his wife, could be available to him and really offer support.

"I was very touched by his concern," Sara explained. "He asked me how much I cared about having children. He said he thought it would be impossible to have both . . . not if I wanted to be the kind of top-notch mother he knew I'd want to be. And, of course, he talked about what a big sacrifice it would be for someone like me to give up having kids. He hadn't been as involved with his kids as he would have liked, but the involvement he *did* have was really important to him.

"Finally, he urged me to assess it all . . . to think long and hard about it and then tell him what conclusion I came to. And if I wanted to be a partner, he assured me that I would be. Obviously, I opted for partnership . . . and I did it with my eyes open. I can't always say I'm happy about the way my work limits my life, but that's the way it is. In fact," Sara concluded, "just a few months ago I had a similar conversation with another woman associate who's coming up for partner. I'm still waiting to hear what her decision will be."

Sara—who is by no definition naive—accepted without challenge the "sage" counsel of her mentor. In fact, she internalized it to the extent that she played it back, whole, when she found herself cast in the position of adviser. She was, somehow, unable to achieve enough distance from her mentor to recognize the hostility (which will be analyzed a bit later) inherent in his advice. And she isn't alone.

Many resourceful women, like Sara, are unable to use their "otherwise good judgment" to determine whether or not the AVBs they find in the workplace are appropriate outside of the workplace. These very same women who manage to look at complicated problems, analyze them, and come up with alternatives all day long, often feel that they have no alternative but to accept the attitudes, values, and behavior of the men around them, and to carry those AVBs over into their personal lives.

Most remarkable is the fact that many women like Sara don't think about questioning advice that their mentors give them, *even when* that advice involves their lives outside of work. This unquestioning posture is, to be sure, out of character. It's so out of character, in fact, that we have to question what's behind Sara's acceptance of so harsh a life sentence. Why was she unable to think creatively about her personal life and, perhaps, come up with some reasonable alternatives to those her mentor offered.

Consider an analogous situation. Imagine a husband in a traditional marriage saying to his wife, "It takes a great deal of time and energy for you to be my wife and I don't believe that you'll have enough time left over for me if we have children. So I don't want to have children." If the wife in that situation wanted to have children, she would most likely have found a way to have them. If she felt that her husband was insecure and worried about a baby rivaling him for attention, she might decide to be very reassuring. Or she might respond with anger and determination. Regardless of how she did it, it's likely that she would question the validity of her husband's judgment.

Yet when men tell women that the pursuit of a career will have to involve the sacrifice of a personal life, their judgment often goes unquestioned. Yes, men have determined the AVBs of the work world, but just how far does their power extend? Perhaps Hollywood had it right: Women are, in this regard, myopic.

Let's examine—as Sara might have examined—the message and information she received from her mentor. First, he told her that she was brilliant. He gave her something: the gift of praise. And it felt good. Then he told her that her future was in her own hands; that if she chose to, she could become a partner. Another gift. It's comforting to be told by someone you trust that you are the master of your own fate.

The second part of her mentor's message, however, makes us regard the two gifts we've just mentioned with some suspicion. This second part of the message involved "payment." Now that Sara's trusted adviser has told her what she is going to get, he's ready to discuss what she, in return, will have to give. And the cost is dear. Rather than demand a pound of flesh, Sara's mentor has exacted several pounds of soul. In essence, he has said, you can only be a partner if you pay for it by signing over your personal life . . . including the potential lives of your unborn children. Such is the stuff of not-so-pleasant fairy tales; and it gets more and more frightening. He goes on to say that *he* does not have to sign over his personal life in order to enjoy success. In fact, *he* finds that he *needs* precisely the sort of supporting environment that she will be obliged to forgo.

Having painted this very unpleasant picture of Sara's future should she decide to opt for partnership, her mentor proceeds to get personal. He begins to talk to Sara the "woman," as opposed to Sara the lawyer. He says that although he has great interest and esteem for her *mind*, he would under no circumstances be interested in her as a woman if she decides to pursue an ambitious career. Any woman who's invested in the sort of career he's invested in simply wouldn't be able to give *enough* to him emotionally.

At the heart of his counsel is the belief that a woman cannot offer *enough* emotional support unless she is willing to make a career of the man in her life. "Pick one," he challenges. "A man like me whom you respect and admire, or your work and a lonely life. Pick one, because you cannot have both."

Make no mistake, the message of Sara's boss—regardless of how friendly he honestly believes he is being—is not friendly. It comes from a childhood system of values—both his and hers—that says "real women" must be exclusively devoted to the task of nurturing their husbands. To the extent that Sara accepts the advice of her mentor, she is also accepting that system; she is accepting the judgment that as long as she is pursuing her ambitious career she is not a "real woman." She deludes herself in thinking that because the advice comes from a man who is successful in the world of work it is substantially different from the AVBs of her own childhood.

It's not difficult to understand why a woman like Sara is locked into the AVBs of the workplace. Those AVBs make her feel good. They bring her gifts like financial independence, a sense of her own very real power and value, to say nothing of the kind of praise that her mentor has taken the trouble to mete out. Let's consider, however, some of the options Sara might have if she were able to open up the lock and not carry the AVBs of the workplace over into her personal life.

For starters, she might have to distance herself psychologically from her mentor in order to question his assumption that any man she could admire and respect would have to be as driven and ambitious as he is. Perhaps Sara might find that a man who is less driven professionally is also less needy personally. Perhaps such a man's expectations of a wife might be different than her mentor's. Or perhaps Sara might find herself more open to a man who can accept the fact that she can give of herself emotionally in a *quality* way, even if she's not available to him *all* of the time. Or she might find a man who is also involved in a time-consuming career but who wants to spend his little bit of leisure time with a woman in a comparable situation, a woman who will be able to understand firsthand the kinds of pressures he experiences in the work world.

There is also the possibility that Sara might find none of the above. That she might find herself in complete agreement with her mentor after having explored, for herself, the message he gave her. The issue here is not so much whether or not Sara's mentor is right or wrong so much as it is Sara's blanket acceptance of him as an authority on issues that involve her personal life. In accepting his judgment Sara is allowing men to define her life, just as women have allowed men to define their lives for centuries.

The mentor has said, essentially, that the only *kind* of woman any man wants is the kind of woman *he* wants, and the fact that Sara finds herself accepting what he says is evidence of the extent to which she's locked herself into a system that is unsympathetic (and even *hostile)* to women.

"Sacrifice"—Romanticizing Deprivation

When we asked Sara how she feels about life without the ongoing presence of an intimate partner, she said that although it's not exactly what she dreamed about as a girl, she's content. "People can't have everything," she explained matter-of-factly, "and I want the kind of career I have. I guess I'm willing to *sacrifice* my personal life in order to have it. Maybe I'll be sorry about it someday, but as of right now I'm content with my decision."

Sara has a good deal of company when it comes to "sacrifice." Nancy F., a medical intern, is one of many women who share Sara's point of view. "I was worried when I decided to go to medical school that I might not get married and have children," Nancy confided with conviction, "but the more I began to think of myself as a *doctor,* the less concerned I was with the other stuff. Women have to be willing to sacrifice some things if they want to have serious careers."

It's important for women to appreciate the extent to which that "sacrifice" is incumbent *exclusively* on them. In 1982 Korn/Ferry International—the management consulting firm we mentioned earlier—published *Profile of Women Senior Executives.* The study was designed as a companion piece to a similar study Korn/Ferry conducted in 1979 which focused

on male executives. (At the time of the first study there simply weren't enough women in high corporate offices to merit
examination.) Consider the following data from that study:

> One of the more significant findings of this survey is
> that 52% of the respondents are unmarried: currently
> divorced (17%), separated (3%), never married (28%),
> and widowed (4%). . . . This is in sharp contrast to the
> 1979 findings for men. Only 4% of them were currently
> divorced, separated or never married and fully 95%
> were married at the time of the study.
>
> Of the women executives who are divorced, 55% state
> that their career was a factor in the divorce.
>
> Sixty-one percent of the women have no children.
> . . . Ninety-seven percent of the males had chil-
> dren. . . ."

The paradigm of a successful man, as reflected in the
Korn/Ferry study, is that of someone with a career plus family; while the successful female counterpart has "sacrifice" as
her model. Of course, men also sacrifice for their careers. But
men don't think about personal sacrifice in the same ongoing
way as women do. Rather, they think in terms of "postpon-
ing" relationships and families until they are securely settled
in a career. The women we interviewed who talked about
"sacrifice" believed—without exception—that they could
not have both a satisfying professional life and a satisfying
personal life. With or without the advice of "aggressive mentors," they all came to view the two life-styles as mutually
exclusive.

The fact that men don't have to make a comparable sacrifice doesn't seem to trouble these women. And it's no wonder. Women's acceptance of sacrifice as both "noble" and a
prerequisite to getting things is consistent with traditional
female AVBs. When women lived by a system of AVBs that
emphasized relationships, they were called upon to sacrifice
their own needs (i.e., personal development) for those rela-

tionships. Mothers sacrificed. Wives sacrificed. It was simply what they did because those relationships were important and serious. They were what mattered.

Basic to traditional male AVBs is the belief that work is important; work is what matters. Women, who were raised with a set of AVBs that embodied self-sacrifice, approach male AVBs with the same willingness to place their own personal needs last. And men—like the aggressive mentor we discussed earlier—reinforce women's inclination to sacrifice.

When we explore what women mean when they talk about "sacrificing for the sake of their careers" from a new, fresh perspective, it seems that they are really talking about punishment. Sacrifice and punishment are, in this context, the same. They are both forms of masochism. The more you sacrifice the more you are being punished. The more you are being punished, either by yourself or by others, the more you feel you are sacrificing. And sacrifice is supposed to be ennobling.

"If I want to be a good, successful doctor," Nancy explained, "I have to be willing to pay the price." "Pay *what* price?" we asked. And what about the men who are Nancy's professional peers? What price do they pay?

When Nancy and other women like her talk about "paying the price," they are talking about doing without the nurturing environment of a personal relationship. That's a formidable deprivation. Sara's mentor said straight out that it was a greater deprivation than he, personally, could bear. Why then do so many career women accept this deprivation as though it were reasonable? Why do they believe that they are, in a sense, deserving of such a hefty punishment?

Nancy, Sara, and other women we interviewed seem to feel guilty for having abandoned or failed by the standards of their childhood AVBs. It is as though they believe they must do penance for not having grown up to be "good girls." Their guilt is intensified because they have devoted themselves to

the AVBs of the "forbidden place," that is, the workplace
men. In a sense these women are trapped between Scyl
and Charybdis. They left a place where they "really" be-
longed and moved into a place where they weren't "really"
supposed to be.

A move like that is scary, whether the women involved are
aware of their fear or not. What could they do to ease the
transition? For starters, they could make themselves more
acceptable by paying their dues. So their membership fee in
this new club became the sacrifice of their personal lives.
Perhaps if they appeased the rulers of this new club with so
substantial a sacrifice they would be accepted as worthy of
their new stations.

Of course, it is demeaning to think of oneself as a willing
partner in the sort of sacrifice we have just laid out. But what
happens is that these women participate unconsciously in the
charade. Rather than perceive their "sacrifice" as the punishment that it is, they regard it in its most lofty incarnation.
Our country was built on sacrifice. The concept is pivotal in
the Judeo-Christian tradition. This is the sort of sacrifice with
which ambitious career women identify. Sadly, however,
these same women cannot view their situation objectively
enough to question why the nature of women's sacrifice is so
different from men's.

When they do gain that objectivity they will be able to
drop the talk of "sacrifice" and question why they are being
"punished." And when that happens, they will be more likely
to find the kind of personal relationships they need to balance their lives.

Denying the Need for Relationships

We said earlier that men traditionally got their identities
from work, and women traditionally got their identities from
relationships. It makes sense, then, that women who brought

kplace into their personal lives would
for identities, in much the way men
many of the women we interviewed did
the process they went one step further.
n who identified with men's AVBs re-
most extreme sense—the AVBs of their child-
hood. They didn't simply say, "I will get my identity from my
work the way men do." They also told themselves, either on a
conscious or unconscious level, that they had to be on guard
to avoid relationships. Relationships were, for them, *dangerous.* A relationship might somehow suck them back into a
system that threatened their identity.

"I have lots of male friends," said Toni L., a thirty-three-
year-old advertising executive who spends between fifty and
sixty hours a week working, "but I don't like to get involved
in really heavy relationships. I just don't have the time and
energy for that sort of thing. They always end up being
messy. And the truth is that I don't really need it either.
Look," she said quite bluntly, "I make a very good salary. I
certainly make enough money to live the sort of life I want to
live. I'm not at all interested in having kids. So what do I need
a relationship for."

We asked Toni about loneliness. "Of course I feel lonely
from time to time," she answered, "but I don't know a single
person who doesn't. I have plenty of married friends who
feel lonely also. I look around and I don't see many relationships that I envy. At least I know that I'm in control of my life.
If I'm happy, I know that it's because I made myself happy.
And if things aren't going well I take full responsibility."

We will, at a later point, discuss intimacy—our need for it
and the consequences of denying that need. For now, it's
important to recognize the bigger context of Toni's denial. In
denying her need for a relationship Toni is embracing the
AVBs of the work world. "Relationships are messy," she said.
Indeed she believes that *emotions* are messy. *Feelings* are
messy. *Vulnerability* is dangerous. Her beliefs go beyond a

rejection of traditional female AVBs to embrace the traditional male AVBs we talked about earlier. When pressed, she went on to equate the need for intimacy with weakness. "I don't need someone to come home to, or a shoulder to cry on," she said defensively. "I can take responsibility for myself."

What, we wonder, is the reward for having no one to come home to? Why not come home and cry on someone's shoulder when you feel like it? Toni may have convinced herself that intimate relationships are not worthy of her valuable time and attention. In doing so, however, she is more likely to end up feeling isolated than independent. She will suffer in the same way as men who confuse intimacy with dependency.

Turning the Tables

Many of the women who carry the AVBs of the workplace over into their personal lives attempt to find traditional relationships like the ones they were raised for, with one significant twist. They reverse roles. Consider the situation of Fay G., a tenured professor of history at a prestigious East Coast university.

Fay's work is very consuming. She publishes books and articles regularly, and when she's finished teaching, writing, guest lecturing, and doing her own political work, she has very little free time. "I'm a human being," she explains, "and I recognize the fact that I have some basic needs, but I don't have time for hearts and flowers. That's why my relationship with Steven is so satisfying. I get what I need without any effort or fanfare."

Fay begins to talk about Steven, a man she's been dating for nearly a year. "The main thing about Steven," she says, "is that he adores me and he's not needy or demanding." What does Fay mean by needy? "Since I met him, nearly two years ago, I don't think I've cooked for him once," she explains. "We go to restaurants. I love it. And if he sees that I need something he'll just go out and buy it.

"Also," she continues enthusiastically, "he adores me. He thinks I'm wonderful. He has a car and that's convenient because he takes the wash to the laundromat. I mean, he'll do anything I tell him to do. On an intellectual level he really isn't my equal—he doesn't have any great insight into my feelings or anything like that—but I have plenty of friends who can provide that for me. Steven provides other things.

"The best thing of all is that because he does free-lance work he gets in at weird hours—eleven or twelve—which is perfect for me. I mean," she laughs, "we spend five or six nights a week together but he comes in, really, just when I would love somebody there . . . after I've done my work, talked on the phone with my women friends, had a swim, taken my singing lessons. It's perfect. He doesn't come on with problems. . . . he's not complicated. . . . I don't have to be a big emotional support. It's all just fun. Like sport."

It's hard to believe that Fay's words are coming out of the mouth of a woman. In fact, her whole perspective is antithetical to the AVBs of her childhood. She sounds much more like the most traditional, chauvinistic man. We have already discussed women's roles in traditional relationships in depth. It was, as we said, their job to see to the needs of their husbands, without in any way interfering with their work. Fay wants a man who will tend to *her* needs—be they practical, emotional, or sexual—without making any demands on her.

Fay, of course, would not tolerate for a moment being in a relationship with a man who spoke about women the way she speaks about Steve. She'd be quick to point out that she was getting the short end of the stick. She doesn't need to think about the fact that Steve may be getting that same short end, however, because she has reduced him to a nonperson. He has become, instead, a housekeeper, a sexual machine, and a "sport."

The issue Fay will eventually have to confront, however, is what the effect of reducing her lover to a nonperson is having on *her*. What does it do to Fay to think about Steve the way she does? It's interesting to note that Fay's personal politics tell her that when there is an oppressed and an oppressor, both parties suffer. She is unable, however, to generalize from her political theorizing to her personal life.

What Fay now calls a "satisfying relationship" has nothing to do with intimacy. It does nothing to address the human needs a genuinely intimate relationship addresses. We will discuss the nature of what we call an intimate relationship in detail later. For the time being it is enough to understand that while it's fine and well for Fay to have a man to sleep with, the fact that she has a sexual outlet does nothing to diminish her need to touch and be touched intimately. Ironically, while women like Fay are losing sight of the difference between those two kinds of touching, many men are beginning to discover it.

Workaholics

At first glance women workaholics and men workaholics seem very much the same. And indeed, they both do go about their lives in a similar way. Most of them are either unable, unwilling, or afraid to stop working. They think of themselves as "work machines," and invest themselves 100 percent in their work, often to the exclusion of a meaningful involvement with anything else: husband, wife, children, hobbies, etc.

It's important, however, for working women to understand how their addiction to work differs from men's. Those differences, which are evident on a number of different levels, were reported recently in the New York *Times,* as follows:

"Mary M. Whiteside, assistant professor of statistics at the

Graduate School of Business of the University of Texas, and her associate, Susan Mosier, surveyed about 1,500 men and women who had received M.B.A.'s from the University of Texas from 1920 to 1980 to determine what impact their education had had on their lives. They found that 52 percent of the workaholic women—women who reported that they worked 50 or more hours a week—were single, compared with 17 percent of the men. Fifteen percent of the women had been divorced compared with 5 percent of the men.

" 'Women workaholics don't reap as many rewards and seem to have more self-doubts than do male workaholics,' Professor Whiteside concluded. 'Women workaholics also seem to pay a greater price for their career devotion.' "

The difference lies in the origins of men's and women's workaholism; and the origins bring us back to the traditional AVBs we discussed earlier.

Men, as we said earlier, were raised to keep a safe emotional distance from other people. This distancing started in early childhood when boys first began to identify with their fathers, rather than their mothers. When they rejected their mothers' identities they also rejected the softness and tenderness they embodied. That softness was replaced, as we discussed, by the male AVBs that dominated their fathers' lives and the world of work. Work was, for men, their manifest destiny.

Of course different men handled all of this distancing in different ways. Those men who later became workaholics responded to their childhood AVBs in a most extreme way. For any number of reasons (conscious and unconscious), they established an exaggerated distance between themselves and the things their mothers represented. The safest way to maintain this distance was to remain in the work world for as much time as possible. If it was good to work, it was better to work more.

Women came to be workaholics in the process of rejecting, rather than fulfilling to the extreme, their childhood training.

They found in the workplace a new kind of recognition and validation that involved their competence, intelligence, independence, and so forth. And that validation felt very good. In fact, it felt so good that some women, like Celia L., the product manager of a large manufacturing company, came to think of the good feelings of a job well done in much the way other women think of the good feelings of an emotionally gratifying relationship. In essence, they came to think of work as the place to find emotional gratification and to assuage their loneliness.

Celia has not taken a vacation in two years. "My boss was dropping travel brochures on my desk," she said, laughing, "but the time never seems right. I don't know how people find the time to get away for vacations. The best I can do is get laid up with the flu for a week, and then I pay for it for months with overload."

Celia's joke would be funnier if she were happier. The more she talks, however, the less inclined we are to laugh with her. "Look," she continued, "work is where I'm happiest. Even in the most stressful office situation I feel good about myself. I like working. I mean, thank God I have my work. Sometimes I feel like my job is the glue that holds my life together. It's there for me. It's reliable. I'm good at it and I'm appreciated by the people I work with. Being productive is very important to me, and at work I can see the results of my efforts. That's a good feeling. Why shouldn't I hold on to it for as long as I can?"

If Celia weren't always busy she might notice the loneliness of her life. Some people go out seven nights a week. Career women can't do that. So they work five nights and go out one or two. For Celia, work is both a source of good feelings and a means of escape and denial. And there's a problem with that.

Celia and other workaholics like her are, in truth, locked into their work. What began as an opportunity has turned, for them, into a new sort of confinement. Celia can flee, through her work, from her need for intimate human contact but she can not successfully *extinguish* that need. The best she can do is keep busy enough so that she won't notice it; and keeping that busy means working all the time.

Regarding Lovers as Competition

Today's career women grew up with mixed messages about competition. Competition against certain people was acceptable at very circumscribed times. Beyond those specifications, however, it wasn't. For example, it was acceptable for girls to compete against each other for the attention of a boy. It was unacceptable, however, for girls to compete against boys. And the unacceptability of such competition increased as girls got older. Competition, according to the traditional AVBs we discussed earlier, was a decidedly masculine trait.

Of course, the ability and willingness to compete is critical to a person's success in the work world. Competition, after all, fuels the American system. It energizes the work world. Women who wanted to succeed at a career found themselves in the position of having to compete against men. Their success hinged, in that regard, on their ability to act counter to the lessons of their childhoods.

For the most part, those women who managed to succeed at a career had no problem competing in the work world. They experienced themselves as "underdogs," and underdogs are traditionally good fighters. Indeed, most of the women we interviewed spoke proudly of long histories of successful competition. They were accustomed, with rare exception, to being at the head of the proverbial class.

Many of these same women who have no problem competing with men in the work world, however, often have a different kind of problem with competition. Some of them, unconsciously, carry their competition into their personal relationships, where it is counterproductive. Irene J., a New York bond trader, is one such woman. She just ended a relationship with a man she'd been dating for nearly a year. "I cared for David very much," she explained, "but I don't think we were really going anywhere. Every time we'd make a breakthrough something would happen that would set us back ten steps."

For example? "Well, I'm very concerned about diet and exercise," Irene said. "To some extent I guess it's a matter of appearance. I like to be in good shape . . . to really look good. But I also think it's a matter of health. I mean, there's no question about the fact that when you eat well and exercise regularly you feel better." Irene paused and looked at us for corroboration. "Well," she continued, "David was ten pounds overweight and couldn't have cared less. I mean, towards the end he'd come running with me on Saturday and Sunday mornings, but he did it to appease me. And he didn't run the distance with me. He'd drop off after a couple of miles and go home to read the paper and eat breakfast. If I weren't on his back about it he'd probably be twenty pounds overweight. He just never seemed to really care about the whole thing the way I did. I just had a date with a man who's a real fitness freak. Obviously, that's not the only thing I care about, but I'll tell you something. It's nice to have someone who surpasses me on that front. It gives me something to aspire to.

"I guess David really didn't care about his appearance as much as I do," Irene continued. "And that bothered me. I mean, it's one thing now when we're both in our late twenties, but ten years down the road it's more important. It's hard to catch up if you let yourself go at this point in life."

All of what Irene said is, no doubt, true. It *is* harder to stay in shape as you get older. The question we ask, however, is what does this have to do with an intimate relationship? Why did Irene have such a hard time separating what she, personally, wants to do from what the man in her life wants to do?

David was not about to keel over. In fact, based on other information Irene gave us it seems that he's healthy and quite attractive, despite his excess ten pounds.

The issue for Irene involves "being right." Irene cares about looking good and being in shape. Therefore, David should. When she said, "He just doesn't care about it the way he *should,*" she really meant that he doesn't care about it the way *she* does. And if he doesn't care about it the way she does, he somehow becomes not *good enough* for her.

Of course Irene would never come out and say, "David isn't good enough for me because he doesn't diet and exercise." But on an emotional level that's what's going on. In order to be worthy of her respect/love/sexual favors a man must be willing to join in a competition with Irene. It doesn't matter so much whether Irene sets the standards or the man in her life sets them. What matters is that there is genuine "striving." When David went running with Irene on weekend mornings she felt that he was simply "humoring" her. It didn't count.

This sort of competition has, as we'll see later, very little to do with an intimate, loving relationship. In fact, it works counter to creating the kind of trusting, relaxing environment in which real intimacy can thrive. In the environment of an intimate relationship Irene would find a nurturing, rather than a competitive, way to convey to David her concern for his health.

Paralleling Work Pressures in Relationships

Many women who have embraced the AVBs of the work world find themselves equating "pressure" with "accomplishment." Some of these women simply don't know how to relax. We discussed the problems of workaholics earlier in this chapter. Other women, however, find that while they are able to leave their specific work behind at quitting time they cannot adjust their pace. They approach their personal lives with the same sense of pressure and at the same frenzied pace that they approach their work lives. Self-imposed pressure in one's personal life often interferes with intimacy. Here again, as we'll see, the issue is one of intimacy versus accomplishment.

One of the women we interviewed was keenly aware of the way the problem manifested itself for her. "I know myself very well," began Marilyn L., the thirty-two-year-old managing editor of a well-known magazine. "I know that I'm the kind of person who works well under pressure. I'm always great at deadline time. I'm organized, I never lose my cool, and I'm a perfectionist. All of those traits have stood me in good stead professionally. But they've taken their toll on my personal life."

Marilyn has been married for two years and loves her husband, Rob, very much. "I really do value my marriage," she told us. "But sometimes I think I drive Rob away. For example, right after we got married we bought a co-op. It was a perfectly nice 'first' apartment. Rob thought we'd take our time and fix it up. But I felt like I wanted it to be fixed up immediately. I hated the idea of living in a place that wasn't really 'done.' So we had lots of fights about it and met somewhere in the middle. It was finished about six months ago: faster than Rob would have liked, and not nearly as fast as I wanted.

"During the time we were fixing up our place," Marilyn continued, "I grew to dread weekends. They'd always end up with us fighting." What did they fight about? "Well, I'd get to the breakfast table Saturday morning with a list . . . sort of an agenda of what had to be done. And Rob would bristle. He'd scream about not wanting to be pressured on his weekends. Which would make me bristle. I'd scream about how the weekends were our only time to get things done. Then he'd finally succumb and he'd sort of drag along with me all weekend feeling very resentful. Then when we'd have to make a decision about something I'd take it very seriously and Rob would tell me I was obsessing. He really felt like it didn't much matter, and that bothered me."

So far, although Marilyn's problem sounds unpleasant, it certainly doesn't sound dangerous. But Marilyn takes issue with that assessment. "No," she explained. "I think that it may be on the verge of getting dangerous. You see, it's only been a few months since we finished fixing up our place, and I've started looking, on the sly, for a house." Marilyn paused and looked a bit embarrassed by what she was about to say.

"I really want to live in a house. I never thought of this apartment as a long-term home. But when I think of all the stress Rob and I went through just fixing this place up it makes me dread the idea of fixing up a home. And then I end up feeling angry at Rob because I can't do what I want to do. The whole thing is becoming kind of messy. And it worries me to think that as soon as I finish one place I want to move on to another . . . without even really sitting back and enjoying what I've done. At work, as soon as we put one month's issue to sleep, we're working on the next. I find that exhilarating. But at home, I find it frightening. It's as though I go about creating pressure in my life when there needn't be any."

Marilyn's anxiety is well founded. There's only so much stress a relationship—even a good relationship—can endure. The fact that Marilyn found her way out of a stressful situation and is planning to dive into an even more stressful situation tells us something about her, and about the way she relates to Rob.

Are Marilyn and Rob making a home together or is Marilyn using her marriage as a showcase of her talents? Why does Marilyn ignore Rob's desire to relax and have low-keyed weekends. That desire of Rob's must be recognized—simply because it's his desire—if Marilyn is to be in an intimate relationship with him. Granted, he could bend to her desire on a given weekend, but the issue here is establishing a life-style.

At work, the pressure Marilyn builds doesn't interfere with the awareness she must have of other people's needs. That awareness is built in to her *modus operandi.* It's an important factor in her success. Indeed, there's nothing objectively wrong with Marilyn's inclination to create pressured situations for herself. There is a problem, however, when the pressure jeopardizes the relationship she values. The problem involves the issue of control. Marilyn is frightened because rather than being in control of the AVBs that work for her in the office, she is at their mercy. And the stakes (i.e., her marriage) are higher than she cares to risk.

All of the women we've discussed in this chapter have, in a sense, been trapped by the success they experience in their work lives. They feel, with good reason, that they owe their success in large part to their powers of observation and to their ability to adapt. They consciously and unconsciously watched successful men; and they consciously and unconsciously altered their own behavior to imitate the behavior of the successful men they observed.

This observation and imitation—regardless of whether it was conscious or unconscious—was hard work. It was an enormously absorbing task. Indeed, it was so absorbing that for a while these same women weren't able to step back and count—or question—their losses. It is only now that they have attained some measurable success in the work world that women are beginning to gain the distance (and security) necessary to stop and assess their overall sense of well-being. What do I have in my life? What am I missing? Why can't I have it all? Such are the questions they are asking themselves.

CHAPTER 4

Being All Things to All People

Work and Love: Pursuing a Total Success Package

As we said earlier, not all of the women we interviewed dealt with their feelings of conflict in the same way. Some women, like those in Chapter 3, attempted to avoid conflict by exchanging their childhood AVBs for the AVBs of the workplace. Many of the women we interviewed, however, went a seemingly opposite route. They decided—either consciously or unconsciously—to compartmentalize. To play each game by its own set of rules; but to play, nonetheless, with the highest standards of each in mind.

The price of playing chameleon in this way is, of course, quite high. One must accept a life fraught with the kind of tension that inevitably accompanies adherence to two conflicting systems of AVBs. Career women, as we said earlier, seem to accept this inner conflict as the price they must pay for pursuing careers. "I guess with all of the talk about superwomen today, I just figured that I'd eventually learn to handle the conflict," said Lois N., a twenty-five-year-old architect at a large Chicago firm, "but I'm beginning to discover the limits of my superpowers."

The super task with which most women have the hardest time—and which gets the least press—is an emotional, rather than a physical, task. Working all day and coming home to cook dinner and nurture a family is not as formidable an accomplishment as making the necessary emotional adjustments—changing AVBs.

Indeed, Lois is beginning to recognize how unrealistic a burden she has assumed for herself. She not only wanted to succeed according to both systems, she wanted to succeed *with flying colors.* Women who manage to have very successful careers usually make higher than average demands on themselves in other areas of their lives as well.

"I guess I was kind of arrogant," Lois said. "I always felt that I could do anything as long as I knew the rules and set my mind to it. If having a career meant I had to switch roles when I left the office I just assumed I'd be able to do it. I figured that if I could manage to lay down my squash racket and play a good set of tennis I could just as easily leave a construction site where I was the boss overseeing fifty construction workers and go home to make a romantic candle-lit dinner and be a little pussycat." Lois laughed and continued. "The only problem is that my candle-lit dinners never worked out right—the way I wished they would. They always ended up with someone being disappointed—either me or the guy I was cooking for. And instead of feeling like a sex kitten I felt like a she-lion with a thorn stuck in my paw."

Lois is not alone. Her desire to succeed simultaneously by the terms of her childhood AVBs and in terms of the AVBs of the workplace—what we call her desire for a "total success package"—is shared by many other career women. Some, like Lois, are left feeling disappointed. Others come out of the conflict feeling frustrated and depressed, or cynical and bitter.

The ultimate resolution for Lois, and for women like her

who attempt to synthesize internally two conflicting systems of AVBs, involves picking and choosing those pieces from each system that are productive and feel good. Before women can do that, however, they must first recognize and acknowledge the manifestations of this conflict; and then they must appreciate the extent to which they have incorporated the conflict in their psyches. The second task, as we'll see, is the more difficult of the two.

Let's look at some examples of both aspects of this problem.

Looking for the "Wrong Kind of Guy"

Women who attempt to pursue a "total success package" often find themselves attracted to what they themselves call "the wrong kind of guy." Consider Shana N., a twenty-three-year-old Princeton graduate who works in Silicon Valley, California—"Computer-land USA."

"On one level I feel best when I'm with a man who really dominates me," she admits, somewhat embarrassed. "There's something about being with a powerful, aggressive man that I find very exciting, and right for me. But those relationships never work out because on another level I want a man who is going to be very sensitive and supportive and tender . . . a man I can really trust. That's what I think of when I think about a husband and a man who will be a father to my children. And I'm slowly beginning to realize that I can't get both kinds of men wrapped up in one gorgeous package."

Shana illustrates her problem by talking about her two most recent relationships. "Not too long ago I was involved with a guy named Harris. He was one of these real computer geniuses. A real dynamo. He designs software . . . some of the biggest-selling stuff on the market today. In fact, he's only twenty-eight and he's already independently wealthy. His royalties could keep him going for the rest of his life.

"I really looked up to Harris," Shana continues, "but he treated me like dirt. He was so wrapped up in himself that my needs always faded into the background. I don't think he ever really listened to me. There were always more pressing matters than my problems. I was involved with Harris for nearly a year, but what did I get out of the relationship?"

Shana recognizes that Harris was a man who met the standards of her childhood AVBs. "The fact that Harris was involved with me made me feel alive. It validated me. When I was growing up my parents were always telling me that whatever I did I'd end up making an important contribution to society. I'd be a real star. And I guess I came to expect nothing less than that in a man. I somehow feel safest with a man I can look up to. A man who dominates me. A man who's stronger than I am. I don't really like to think of myself as a masochist, but sometimes I wonder."

Shana is not a masochist. She doesn't enjoy being treated poorly by men. If she did, she wouldn't have ended her relationship with Harris. She gets into those relationships for a number of reasons.

First, she's still hooked into her childhood AVBs to the extent that she pursues hierarchical relationships. When she is with a man who dominates her she feels that she has succeeded by the terms of those AVBs. We discussed this phenomenon in depth earlier.

But more important, when Shana is with a man like Harris she feels relieved of the high expectations that were always placed on her. "When I was a kid," Shana explains, "my parents always told me that I was special . . . that I'd do something special with my life . . . something really out of the ordinary. Well, when I was with Harris I felt like just being the woman in his life was exceptional. And I think that sort of let me off the hook of having to do anything too spectacular on my own.

"I left Harris," Shana continues, "because I really felt lonely the whole time I was with him." Clearly, Shana's relationship with Harris didn't meet her emotional needs for intimacy. "At that point I had a good friend named Jeff whom I worked with. All the time I was living with Harris, Jeff and I used to have lunch together, or go to movies when Harris was busy. I really liked Jeff. When Harris and I split up Jeff and I began sleeping together. I told myself, 'This is the kind of man you should be with.' But there was no magic. Even though I like Jeff and respect him, I just never felt really safe and secure with him. I never felt that he could take care of me."

Jeff was, indeed, gentle, supportive, trustworthy, and encouraging. But he was not a man who could take care of Shana by fulfilling the expectations she internalized as a child. As long as Shana remained involved with Jeff, she'd have to take care of fulfilling those expectations by herself. And for her, that was a scary prospect.

Confronting the AVBs of one's childhood head-on and fitting them in with one's adult aspirations is, as we'll see, a difficult process, and one that Shana has avoided. This discrepancy of expectations has resulted, for Shana, in a series of relationships without a future—relationships that fuel a growing frustration and depression.

She wants a man who will take care of her and relieve her of the burden of being independent, and she wants a man who will encourage her to pursue her own independent ambition. She's right when she says she won't find them both wrapped up in one. She cannot find one person who will satisfy the expectations of both sets of AVBs.

In fact, Shana will not find a satisfying relationship until she first examines why she feels anxious around men who are both powerful and directive. She'll discover that implicit in her need for a powerful man is a lack of belief in herself: in her own independent success and potential.

Seeing Yourself as a Threatening Woman

Women who are locked into conflicting systems of AVBs often have a hard time enjoying any aspect of their success. When they succeed by one set of standards they fail by the other, and their focus is more often on their failure than on their success. Those women we interviewed who were most successful and powerful, for example, often talked about how their success made them seem off limits to most men . . . threatening and unapproachable.

Frances G., who heads up her own public relations firm, is one such woman.

"I earn nearly $150,000 a year," she says, "and that doesn't even take into account all of the benefits of my expense account and tax write-offs. But somehow I just don't feel like such a success. Every time I go home to visit my parents I bring all sorts of elaborate gifts hoping that if I bring lots of evidence of my success I'll somehow be able to avoid all of the usual questions about why I haven't 'settled down.' The fact is that I'd like to be settled down. I don't think I'd like to be quite settled down the way my mother means it, but I'd certainly like to have a man in my life . . . and maybe even a kid . . . although I'm kind of late for that.

"In the context of my parents' home, a forty-five-year-old woman with no permanent man in her life is a freak, and regardless of what I do, whenever I leave their house—which fortunately is halfway across the country—I feel that I'm some sort of freak rather than a great American success story."

Frances is not the only woman who described herself as feeling like a "freak." We'll talk about that feeling in more detail later. "I'm in a difficult situation," Frances concludes. "It's hard for a woman in my position to meet men. I think most men find me too threatening."

There is, without question, some truth to her observation. Many men find successful women threatening. Indeed, the majority of women we talked to mentioned the possibility that men might find them threatening. Men are, after all, subject to the AVBs of their own childhoods; and they were, like women, trained for hierarchical relationships. But women cannot control the way men cope with *their* childhood AVBs. Women can only attempt to cope with their own.

Frances needs to ask herself whether or not *she* believes that her career success is in any way a real threat to men. Does she think of herself as less "feminine" because she's successful? Does she think her success will in some way diminish the value of a man with whom she might be involved? Does she measure men against herself in order to determine their worth? Most women do, and it's no wonder. Their perspective reaches way back into their childhoods.

Frances needs to explore her own concepts of masculine and feminine. If she believes that the only viable relationship is, necessarily, hierarchical in structure, then it's likely that she perceives herself to be a threat. Somehow, through her words or actions, she will present herself to men as the threat she unconsciously believes herself to be. The voice of her childhood AVBs tells her that strong women pose a threat to men. That voice governs her behavior and becomes a self-fulfilling prophecy.

If, on the other hand, she is really looking for a reciprocal relationship with a man, she'll find a way to let him know that she is not a threat. The fact that a man perceives Frances as threatening need not mean that she *is actually* threatening. It simply means that the man is frightened. She may be able to help him deal with that fear. She may not. But she will certainly be on the right track if she makes the effort.

Feeling Like a Freak

We mentioned earlier that many of the women we spoke with said that they often felt like "freaks." It's a strong word, and they used it because their efforts to satisfy the AVBs of both men and women left them feeling disenfranchised from both systems.

Helen L., a young woman in her last year of medical school had a particularly painful experience along those lines. "I once overheard two interns talking in the doctor's lounge at our hospital," she recalled. "They were talking about how little time they had to meet women . . . the usual stuff about how hard a doctor's life is and how horny they were. A friend of mine, Sue, walked by them on her way to make rounds and stopped to say hello. The guys were very friendly, but as soon as she left the room one of them cracked a joke about Sue's being 'vaguely reminiscent of a female.' The other quipped about female medical students being 'not men and not women, but a whole new gender unto themselves.'

"I know that not all of my male classmates feel that way about us, but a lot of them do. And a lot of them don't even realize the extent to which they feel that way. I suppose I should have had a 'screw you' attitude about all of this but the truth is I just wanted to go hide. I felt as though I had a hole in the pit of my stomach. It really hit a nerve."

The "nerve" to which Helen referred is connected to her feeling of womanliness. Despite her own intellect which argues otherwise, on an emotional level Helen believes some of what she overheard. She believes that she is not competent at being a "real" woman. And she wants to hide because she is ashamed of her failure. She feels like a "freak"—neither male nor female.

Robert White notes in the *Nebraska Symposium on Motivation* that shame is always associated with incompetence.

"It occurs," he says, "when we cannot do something that either we or an audience—like our parents [or, in Helen's case, her classmates]—thinks we should be able to do."

Helen desires to be the kind of woman that her male classmates will recognize as a "real" woman. Her decision to be a doctor, however, seems to cancel out for her the possibility that she might offer pleasure to men. And she wants very much to be a doctor. Unfortunately, the pleasure she might otherwise experience from having become a doctor is attenuated by her unconscious belief that being a doctor interferes with being a "real" woman. She wants both, and suffers as a result.

How does Helen suffer? She alternates between anger and depression. Anger assumes the problem lies *outside*. Depression assumes that the problem lies *within*. When Helen feels angry she identifies "men" as the problem: They don't notice her; they don't ask her on dates; they don't appreciate what she, as a woman, has to offer. On the other hand, when Helen is depressed she believes, unconsciously, that she has failings as a woman and that the men around her are all aware of those failings. Indeed, her feelings of shame are a symptom of her depression. She is *ashamed* of her failings.

Those same feelings of shame also interfere with her relationships with men. When Helen feels that she is a failure as a woman she experiences herself as being needy and helpless in the realm of relationships. She expects the men with whom she is involved to validate her "womanliness," but, of course, none of them succeeds in doing so. Men cannot do for Helen what she must do for herself. Until Helen redefines femininity to suit her adult aspirations—until she recognizes and addresses the conflict she perceives between being "womanly" and being a doctor—she will continue to feel vulnerable to the bantering of her classmates.

The Buildup of Anger

Women who attempt to be successful by the terms of their childhood and workplace AVBs often feel the buildup of anger as they get older. The older they get the less energy they have to deal with the pressure their conflict creates.

Nora G., the sixty-three-year-old director of a private school in Dallas, is the oldest woman we interviewed. "I think the reason I got as far as I did professionally is because I pushed myself. I'm not afraid of responsibility and never have been. I know how things should be done, I try to hire people who will meet my standards, and if they don't work out I either train them or do the job myself. Until recently I've felt very good about myself. I think I've even felt lucky. I've always liked my life. I've enjoyed work and I have a very solid marriage and homelife. But there's been a change in the last year or so."

The change of which Nora speaks involves her feelings at both work and at home. "I've been very touchy lately," she says. "For example, I feel put upon when one of the faculty comes to me with a problem she hasn't even tried to solve herself. In the past I would have been happy to do both her work and mine. But now I feel angry, and when I get home I bring my anger with me. I've been harboring this great desire to come home at night, curl up in a big chair with a book, and just disappear. My kids, of course, are grown and out of the house, but my husband is still there, and I need to be there for him."

Nora thought she'd wait a while and the feeling would pass. But that hasn't happened. In fact, people are beginning to notice a change in her, and that concerns her. "A few weeks ago," she recalls, "one of the women I've worked with for years asked me to join her for lunch. We sat down and she looked at me in this very intense way she has, and asked if I were all right. She said I seemed jumpy and angry. Well, I was shocked and also kind of worried. I began to worry that I was, perhaps, falling down on the job. As you get older, you worry more about being replaced. That night when I got home I was very preoccupied by a lot of things at the office. Mark was talking about something or other while I was making dinner, and the truth is that I wasn't really listening to him. I was thinking about lunch and a Board of Director's meeting I had to prepare for. Actually, I was worrying about whether or not the Board had noticed the change in me also. Of course, it didn't take Mark long to notice that I wasn't really there for him and he asked me what was bothering me."

Nora has always been hesitant to trouble Mark with her problems. "I'm old fashioned," she explains. "I feel like I have to take care of everything at home. I have to protect him." Those feelings were heightened a few years ago when Mark had a coronary.

"When Mark asked me what was happening I just told him I was preoccupied with work. I didn't get into how pressured I'd been feeling, or how put-upon I feel these days. And I certainly didn't tell him that I was worried about losing my job. What for? He'd think I was crazy!" she says, throwing her hands up in the air. "I have to think about work all day. I don't need to bring my problems home.

"But I worry," she adds, "about a growing distance between us."

Nora thinks that her anger is something new, when, in fact, it isn't new at all. She identifies her problem as being unable to say no; but the real problem is that she cannot let go of the image of herself as being perfect: of having all the answers at work and being the perfect wife at home. And the struggle involved with maintaining this self-image instead of paying more heed to her own emotional needs is beginning to wear her down. In her weakened condition she is slipping off her pedestal, and it's scaring her more than it's scaring anyone else.

Let's focus on the problems Nora is having at home in order to understand how they connect to the struggle we've just described. Nora is afraid to talk to Mark about her anger for three reasons. First, she wants to protect him. Second, she doesn't believe he could do anything to help. And third, she doesn't want to bring the office home.

Nora's desire to protect her husband is a manifestation of the AVBs of her childhood. A wife is a nurturer . . . a protector. Nora believes that if she eases up on that role the slightest bit she will be punished. On an emotional level Nora seems to believe that her sharing her problems with Mark will kill him—will bring on another heart attack. That will be her punishment for being less than perfect.

All of these fears do not acknowledge the fact that Mark is asking Nora—literally—to tell him what's wrong. In effect, by dancing around his questions Nora is closing Mark out of her life. And there's every likelihood that Mark experiences as much pain from being closed out of his wife's life in that way as he would by hearing about her problems. Mark is not being spared suffering because Nora is keeping her problems under wraps. He's simply suffering in a different way.

Nora's assumption that Mark couldn't help with the problem may or may not be correct. The fact is that although Mark has never taught or worked in a school setting, he has spent more than thirty years being married to a woman who has. He might have picked something up during that time. And in his own work—he is a retired lawyer—he has had many dealings with boards of directors. He has his own life-time of business experiences upon which to draw. Most probably, Mark is better equipped to help Nora than Nora is equipped to ask for help. Nora needs to believe that no one—not even Mark—can help her. She equates "serving others" with strength and seeking gratification for herself with weak-ness. And she can't allow herself to be weak lest her world fall apart: her husband will die and she'll lose her job. "Aren't selfish children always punished?" is what she feels.

Finally, Nora fights against polluting the sanctity of their home with the problems of the workplace. Of course, the truth is that Nora's home is polluted whether she *talks* about her work problems or not. The fact that she carries the problems within her head means that those problems have crossed the threshold with her. If she were able to talk about them at home, she might recognize that her needs are legitimate. That is an awareness that would bring relief.

Instead, Nora feels angry most of the time and has fantasies of escaping . . . of sitting in a comfortable chair and disappearing. At this point in her life she can think of no other way out.

But there is. Until now, Nora's style of handling pressure has come directly from her childhood AVBs. She has coped with pressure while maintaining her standards of perfection. But that means of coping is no longer working. Nora's decision on what she can or cannot handle cannot be rooted in old formulas that have nothing to do with what she actually feels inside herself . . . right now.

"It's funny," Nora says as the interview is coming to a close. "I just don't know when it's going to be time for *me*. Time for Nora. There are things I want to do. Books I want to read. Thoughts I need time to think. When I was younger I always assumed the time would eventually come. When I was forty I figured I had plenty of time. When I was fifty, I thought there'd be time. Now that I'm well into my sixties, I'm beginning to realize that there may never be time." Indeed, there won't be time for Nora unless she creates that time.

"There Are No Men Out There"

Many of the women we interviewed who were not in relationships expressed their hopelessness by saying things like "There are no men out there," or "All the good ones are taken," or "All the good ones are gay," or "I only meet the dregs." In a later chapter we'll discuss the criteria these women draw upon when they judge the men they meet. For now, however, we need to look at their feeling of hopelessness and analyze how they handle it.

We can start with June F., a businesswoman in her mid-thirties. "My closest friend just got married," she explained, "and although I'm really very happy for her, the fact is that I feel like I've been pretty much left behind. Sometimes I feel like life is passing me by. It's an awful feeling. Worse even than being the last kid picked for a softball team because you *never* even get picked."

Why does June think she hasn't been able to find a man? "Who knows?" she said. She runs through what seems to be a familiar song to her. Indeed, we've all heard the lyrics before, and she sounds bored with her recital of them. "I'm too much of a threat. I won't demean myself for a man. I won't go to bars. I'm too tall. I'm too smart." She paused and summed it all up with the great familiar refrain: "What can I tell you? There just aren't any men out there."

Most of the single women we interviewed sum up their problem with the same refrain. "There are no men out there." "What about the man your friend just married?" we asked June. "It was a fluke," she answered. Then she laughed in anticipation of what she was about to say. "Anyway, he was the last one. Now all the good ones are taken for sure."

The fact that men and women get married every day seems to be evidence that there are men "out there." It may be difficult, because of logistics or cultural inhibitions, for career women to meet the kind of men they want, but there are, to be sure, men "out there." So what's the significance of the familiar refrain?

Essentially, when women say that there are "no men out there," they are attempting to gain some comfort by lumping all men together as one great impersonal generic mass, and then blaming this anonymous heap of mankind for their loneliness. It hurts less to think about "men," than it does to think about a specific man. And whatever hurts less in the short run is easier.

From a psychological perspective, blaming others is the external manifestation of a process called *projection*. When we have a problem from which we want relief we *project* the problem onto other people. In fact, blaming others is one of our most primitive means of defense. Children do it all the time because they have such limited resources with which to deal with their difficulties.

For example, if a child feels like a "creep" because she wasn't invited to another child's birthday party, she might say, "I wouldn't want to go to your party anyway because *you're* a creep." Once or twice her projection might ease her pain, but if she continues to miss out on birthday parties she's probably going to want to figure out a way to get herself invited . . . something more productive than blame.

"There are no men available," June said to herself. "That is why there's no man in my life." In fact, June needs to question her own *emotional* availability. By lumping men together the way she does, she interferes with the possibility of getting together with just one man in an intimate way. She is sabotaging herself. But why?

In fact, on an unconscious level June does not really make herself available to men because she has deviated from her childhood AVBs and pursued a career. Many women who deviated from their childhood AVBs in order to pursue careers—but who still hold on to those AVBs for their emotional gratification—believe on an emotional level that career women are not available to men. They say, for example, "There are no men out there." Translation: "I am not *out there* for a man. I am, instead, *in here* . . . in my career."

It's enormously significant when grown-up women, who have so recently struggled for adult status, still rely on such a primitive means of coping with their environment. It indicates that, despite any protestations, they still feel considerable powerlessness. Their choice of defense reveals their emotionality: The medium is the message. June doesn't feel independent and powerful when she thinks about a relationship with a man, even though in other areas of her life she is an extraordinarily resourceful woman. The conflicting systems of AVBs that she carries around with her are her handicap. They leave her feeling crippled.

The women we've discussed above experience a painful conflict between career success and their desire for fulfilling personal lives. Their efforts to resolve this conflict—as discussed throughout this chapter—don't work, and often leave these extraordinarily talented women feeling that their career accomplishments are the source of their pain.

The issue, as we'll see in Chapter 5, is not the work itself; rather, it's the belief that success in the workplace is somehow in conflict with being a woman.

CHAPTER 5

Forging New Identities

Femininity—Then and Now

Clearly, women today are living in a state of transition. That transition was exemplified in the conflict experienced by the women we've discussed until now. They are leaving behind a system of AVBs that provided them a well-defined, secure path for the rest of their lives. That system told them precisely what their goals would be and what they had to do to achieve them. When women started challenging these goals—goals that involved defining themselves in terms of others—they found themselves facing uncharted terrain. It was exciting, but proved to be frightening as well; particularly when the attainment of new goals—i.e., success in the workplace and autonomy—left these same women *still* unsatisfied.

Ambitious, achieving career women, as we'll see in this chapter, have been unable to find a comfortable way to acknowledge and satisfy their needs for self-actualization as well as for intimacy. Women discovered that they had both of these needs and that they would have to forge a new set of values to address them. In essence, they would need to forge new identities.

It's important to emphasize, however obvious it may seem, that women are not the only ones affected by their emergence as independent people. As women experiment with new roles, so do men—either willingly or reluctantly. "People talk about women's problems all the time, but the adaptive stress men undergo when their wives take on a career has been virtually lost sight of," says Preston Munter, a psychiatric consultant to Itek Corporation. "Even if you could postulate an ideal man and an ideal marriage, this would be a difficult transition to make."

Of course, one of the reasons that less attention has been paid to the transition men have had to make in light of the Women's Movement is that men have, traditionally, held a position of power. Their efforts to deny women access to that power cast them in the role of oppressors and women in the role of the oppressed. When people look at any change in the status quo their sympathies are usually directed more toward the oppressed than the oppressor.

Although men, *as a group,* have been cast as villains by the Women's Movement, they are, as Dr. Munter points out, also victims. There is no question but that they've suffered from the limitations of their gender identities in much the way women have suffered from theirs. Indeed, many men are just beginning to recognize the ways in which they've suffered.

Frank J., a successful corporate lawyer, is one such man. "When my son was fifteen a client gave me a box to the World Series," he began. "I'd spent the better part of my son's first fifteen years at the office doing what I thought I should be doing. Seeing to it that I made partner so that we could live in a good neighborhood with good schools. The usual stuff. Well, here I was with tickets to a ball game that I figured any fifteen-year-old boy would be thrilled to get. I came home bursting with the news and he told me he was busy that

Saturday . . . that he was getting together with some guys in his band to rehearse for a concert.

"I was pretty upset . . . for lots of reasons. First of all, I was upset that my boy wasn't as excited about the tickets as I assumed he'd be. And I guess I had some fantasy about this father and son day at the ball game. I mean, I could have gone into the office and worked on Saturday. Or I could have played golf. But here I was going to take the time to be with him and he wasn't jumping at the opportunity.

"Later that night my son came over to me and said, 'Dad, if you really want to go to the ball game with me I'll see if I can change the rehearsal.' So I said, 'Great,' and he changed the rehearsal. I was really moved by his offer. I mean, the whole thing started with my thinking I was doing something for him, and it ended up with his really doing something for me.

"We went to the ball game together," Frank continued, "and had a pretty good time. But when I came home that night I felt, for the first time, that I really didn't know my own child. I didn't know how to read him. I felt awkward when I tried to think of things to talk about. In fact, I think he knew more about how to be a real comfort to me than I did about how to make him happy. All of that 'feeling' stuff was always my wife's job. And I must admit that I don't feel very good about that."

Frank is not a villain. He is, in a real sense, a victim of the concept of "good fathering" with which he was raised. And both he and his son have lost out as a result. Today, Frank is struggling to make up for lost time. And his new models for parenting are his wife and, interestingly, his son. Dr. Diana Zuckerman, a clinical psychologist, directed a five-year study (beginning in 1977) of students from Barnard, Bryn Mawr, Mount Holyoke, Radcliffe-Harvard, Smith, Vassar, and Wellesley to measure how goals, values, and interests of students changed during college. Students responded to more than one hundred questions in five areas: career and education goals, family background, factors that motivated them to pursue various careers, attitudes toward college, and life priorities in fifteen to twenty years.

"The most interesting finding was how little female and male students differ today," said Dr. Zuckerman. "For example, more than ninety percent of both women and men plan to obtain graduate degrees. Ninety-two percent would like to marry and eighty-eight percent would like to have children."

With regard to "life priorities," the *Seven College Study* found that both men and women placed a high priority on family life. Only 10 percent of those surveyed said they planned to have full-time jobs when their children were infants. One third of the thousand men surveyed from Harvard and Vassar—the only schools included in the survey that admitted men—said they would prefer to stay home or work part-time while their children were preschoolers. One third said they expected their time with their spouses would be their top priority in fifteen to twenty years. These findings are particularly interesting when you take into consideration that many of the men questioned came from Harvard. If Harvard, which has traditionally provided us with leaders (in industry, politics, medicine, etc.), is, in fact, turning out a less ambitious, less achievement-oriented kind of man, it is, indeed, very significant.

New Models

In the process of developing new gender identities, men and women have a great deal to learn from each other. As women begin to emerge from the oppressive limitations of their traditional sexual stereotyping, it becomes critical that they recognize the limitations of traditional male stereotyping as well, lest they merely trade one set of limitations for another, as we discussed in Chapter 3.

How do women avoid the pitfalls to which men have fallen prey? They make an effort to notice change: men's and their own. It's important for Frank's wife, for example, to recognize and respect the kind of feelings Frank is having about his success or failure as a father; and it's important for her to try to keep an open dialogue . . . not only for her husband's benefit but for her own as well.

Traditional sexual stereotypes, like all stereotypes, are by definition generalities. They provide us, however, with valuable information in that they tell us the kind of behavior our culture reinforces. Although there has been a great deal of discussion of late about inherent genetic differences in the way boys and girls develop such characteristics as aggression, for example, it wouldn't be productive to focus on that for our purposes. Genetically determined behavior is not subject to change; and change is what concerns us.

Both men and women need to focus on their potential for being similar. Their similarity lies in their feelings. Frank's wife, for example, doesn't feel isolated from her children but she probably can identify with the pain Frank is experiencing. She may even feel isolated from her husband, in which case she could validate his feelings by telling him. "I know what you're feeling," she might say. "And I know that it's painful. Sometimes I feel that way about us."

Villains or victims, men will continue to be the individuals with whom heterosexual women build their intimate relationships; and as such, their individual struggles will always touch critically on women's lives. Men and women grow to be different from each other by absorbing the AVBs of the world around them. Today, those AVBs are changing. Those changes were reflected in the *Seven College Study.* The evidence seems to indicate that both men and women are "unlearning" their differences. In many ways—particularly for older people—that kind of un-learning is much more difficult than was the original learning process.

Older men—men who were already adults as the Women's Movement got under way—have a harder time adjusting to the changes that are expected of them than do younger men.

Despite the fact that Frank was more absorbed in his work than his family, Frank's wife had her own meaningful career, and Frank's son grew up in a world that was different from the one in which his father grew up. When a man's wife brings in a significant portion of the family income he's more likely than not to take a more active role around the home. To be sure, he may not do as much as his wife does, but chances are he does more than his father did. Men's behavior is changing, and along with this behavioral change is a gradual change in attitudes and values.

As the gap between male and female behavior narrows, men and women will have easier access to each other's feelings. They will have more opportunity for empathy—more shared experiences—and, as a result, begin to know each other better. The *Seven College Study* and the experiences of men like Frank seem to indicate that men are beginning to identify with women and female AVBs in the home in much the way women identified with men and male AVBs in the workplace.

When a man like Frank has his feeling validated he begins to notice the limitations of the old system—a system that locked him into the position of provider and encouraged him to pay little attention to his feelings and his children. Those men who have taken the time to stop and look at themselves are beginning to notice that something is wrong. And those men who haven't yet stopped will find, in the next ten years, that they are forced to.

Today, 24.5 million wives, or roughly fifty percent of the nation's married women, are working or looking for work. And that number is growing. When a man who is blindly locked into his childhood AVBs applies for a loan and finds himself face to face with a female bank officer, he will have to stop and take notice. And he'll have to relate to her as he would to a male bank officer. He'll have to tell her his needs and rely on her professional judgment. Such interactions will subliminally affect the way he relates to other women in his life, women like his wife and daughters.

Consider the following situation in the life of one couple—Greg and Liz. Despite the fact that they genuinely have each other's best interests at heart and are willing to work with each other, the going can often be quite rough. They are motivated, however, to work things out because they both believe that the going would be even rougher if they didn't have each other for support.

Changing the Old Guard—Greg and Liz

Greg J., a successful PR man, prides himself on the fact that he's a feminist. "I supported the Women's Movement before it was even a movement," he said. "I think I'm as sensitive as any man to the issues women have to deal with. My wife, Liz, has a very demanding job as a magazine editor. She's always working late with deadlines and such, and I think we pretty much share equally at home . . . with the kids and all." Liz is quick to agree with her husband's evaluation. "But I'll tell you," Greg said, shaking his head, "even with all of my efforts I still screw up on lots of things."

For example? "Well, a few months ago I noticed that Liz was coming home from work very flat. She's usually a buoyant person. She's always got lots of things to talk about. But all of a sudden it seemed like there was nothing. Finally, she burst into tears one night and said that she didn't know what to do. That she felt like she wanted to run away."

"I hadn't planned to fall apart that way," Liz explained. "I hate that sort of thing. But I got home and felt suddenly overwhelmed by everything. The office. The kids. The house. Everything."

"I got on the phone," said Greg, "and called a friend who took the kids to MacDonald's, and Liz and I went to a local restaurant that we both really like, had a few drinks, and she began to talk. It seemed that there had been changes at the office. One of these big communications conglomerates acquired her publishing firm and all these MBA types were making their presence known. I knew about the takeover, of course, but I had no idea how it was affecting Liz."

"Everyone was feeling kind of uptight," Liz said, "and I was no exception. I started to notice that I wasn't getting the kinds of assignments I used to and I was worried. On that day, specifically, a series of articles I had wanted to do was killed."

"She thought, maybe, she was going to be squeezed out, and the thought of that was driving her crazy," Greg recounted. "In fact, she said that the scariest thing was that her work was beginning to be affected. She just didn't feel like she was putting out good copy.

"Liz asked me if I thought she was being paranoid and I said that I didn't think she was being paranoid, but I also didn't think she was being squeezed out. I thought she, and probably most of the other people at her office, were having a problem with the transition. Then I told her about an analogous situation I had had years earlier when I worked at a giant public relations firm and thought I was losing my biggest client. I told her the whole story and how I handled it and suggested that if she did something similar she'd probably feel better. It involved a sort of civilized confrontation with my boss. Anyway, Liz seemed much better, but as soon as we got home she began to cry again. We were right back where we'd started from. And I found myself kind of angry."

Greg shook his head. "There I was, as helpful as I knew how to be. I spent three hours with Liz after my own hard day at the office. I told her exactly how to do it. I thought everything was going so well, and then it all fell apart. I mean, we've both got the same thing in mind: We want her to get over the problem and begin enjoying her job again. But when it was all said and done my help seemed to make her feel worse. I felt like saying, 'What the hell do you want of me?' "

What happened? People who have been helped don't feel worse after the help than they did before. Clearly, Liz's distress at the end of this carefully planned evening was an indication that she didn't *feel* helped, even though Greg wanted very much to help her. Something had been fumbled in the process.

We asked Greg how he felt when Liz asked him for help. "I felt terrific," he answered thoughtfully. "I mean, here was my wife, obviously having a hard time, and I was going to make it easier for her. She came to me for help and I really felt like I wanted to be there for her."

Then we asked Liz about how she felt that night? "Awful," she said. "I felt like my carefully constructed career was about to collapse and I needed to be rescued."

We explored further by asking Greg about the analogous problem he had had years earlier. He answered with the kind of passion and energy people have when they discuss something that happened to them a day or so earlier. In fact, his problem had occurred nearly a decade ago, but it had been so intense that to this day it still triggers an immediate emotional response.

The intensity of Greg's problem had, in fact, led him to overidentify with his wife. Rather than help her get in touch with how *she* might deal with the issues that were causing her great unhappiness, he told her exactly what to do. What he did in a similar situation had worked very well for him because it grew out of his own confrontive, take-charge style of dealing with things. Liz, however, didn't feel comfortable with Greg's style. His solution wouldn't work for her, and when she recognized that she became overwhelmed by a number of feelings.

"First, I felt guilty," she explained. "Here I was with this wonderful husband who was willing to take the time to help me and what's my response? A rejection of his effort. Ingratitude. Second," she went on, "I felt angry. I wasn't sure just why I felt angry, and I'm still not, but I think it was because I thought that when Greg and I talked everything would somehow be taken care of . . . and I'd feel better. And instead of feeling better, I felt worse." Finally, Liz felt impotent. When Greg didn't "make it all better," she felt particularly hopeless. There was nothing anyone could do. So she dissolved into tears again.

Although Liz knew that her *save me* desires were not reasonable—that, in fact, she is an extremely competent woman who has managed to move up within her own industry based on her own talents—the truth is that she felt helpless and wanted some magic. She felt like a little girl, living in the system of her childhood, waiting for her Daddy to scare away the bogeyman and make it all better.

Greg picked up on Liz's wish to be saved before they went out to dinner. He picked up on it with that part of him that, from childhood on, had associated that being a *real* man meant being able to *save* women. Intellectually, he didn't recognize that he was acting on that childhood part of himself. He believed that he was helping Liz out, rather than attempting to *save* her. Despite the fact that they are in a relationship in which they want to be equals, they were dealing with a crisis, and during crises people often regress to earlier ways of dealing with problems.

Liz's helplessness made Greg feel a need to be *bigger*. When she rejected his help, Greg felt as if his entire sense of himself had been knocked down—he felt small and weak and useless. In fact, he felt like a child. He recalled, bitterly, how his mother had always chided him about being "good at everything except the things that matter." Indeed, Greg felt like a failure at the job that matters most to him: being a man. And his own painful "failure" became his focus. In an effort to escape his own pain he withdrew from Liz and her struggle.

So what started out as a loving effort, ended with anger and some despair on everyone's part.

The Damsel in Distress Trap

What Greg and Liz experienced was a clash of two systems. Intellectually, each of them wanted to work through the problem by calling on a system of AVBs they had developed together to replace their childhood AVBs. Greg had been married before to a helpless, dependent woman who was unconflicted about wanting to be taken care of. He knew that sort of relationship didn't work for him—that it made him angry and want to withdraw. In fact, it was his reaction to his first marriage that got him involved with Liz—a fiercely independent, ambitious woman.

Liz had never been married before and maintained that one reason she had held off on matrimony for so long was that she couldn't find a man who could tolerate—indeed, love— her ambition and independence. When she met Greg she recognized that he had a great respect for all the things she had worked so hard to attain. Their marriage was based on the idea that they would relate consistently within these mutually accepted values.

Yet when Liz felt her work crisis reach a peak she approached Greg with a classic *save me* plea—the damsel in distress: "I don't know what to do. I can't stand it anymore." And then she began to cry. She recovered from her crying and continued appealing to Greg's childhood system from somewhere way back in her own. "Everything is falling apart. What should I do?"

A woman's "save me" cry will, almost always, invoke the superhero in the man who loves her. Before Greg and Liz had their dinner, Greg might just as well have ducked into a phone booth to don a Superman outfit. Both he and Liz expected him to exhibit some superpowers.

We can't really rid ourselves of our childhood AVBs, nor should we try. They are part of who we are, and efforts to rid ourselves of them usually result in more denial than purging. The issue is not so much ridding oneself of one's childhood AVBs as it is recognizing when they make us act against our own best interests. This recognition comes after you develop a sense of what your best interests—or your *adult aspirations* —are.

If Liz had been able to act from her adult aspirations, she would have been able to ask for help, rather than salvation. And Greg would have been able to think about how he could be most useful rather than how he could "make it all better" for his wife.

Let's consider some alternative interactions Greg and Liz might have had that would have better served their adult systems. In the first alternative Liz does a good deal of thinking and work on her own before she approaches Greg. She comes to him with a plan and asks his reactions to it. Ultimately, *she* will make the decision about what she does; and she will accept the responsibility of that decision.

In the second alternative Liz might have approached Greg with her emotions—fear, insecurity, etc.—and told him why she felt the way she did. Greg would then be in a position of offering Liz emotional validation—of being there for her— without bearing the responsibility of making her pain go away.

Alternative #1

In order to elicit Greg's help, rather than demanding salvation, Liz needed to give a good deal of thought to her problem and break it down into "do-able" increments.

Suppose Liz had said, "I've been depressed by how little good material I get to work on lately and feel like I'm going to have to do something about it. I've written down a series of article ideas and targeted the market for them, and I've developed a few of them in detail. Would you take a look at them for me and set aside a time for us to talk? I'll feel much better giving them to my boss if I've tried them out on you first."

If she had approached Greg this way, he might have entered their evening feeling committed to discussing Liz's ideas. His goal for the evening would have been "Tonight I want to be *useful* to Liz. I can be useful to her if I give serious attention to her work and react to it honestly." Rather than "Tonight I have to come up with the solution to Liz's problem." The difference between "saving" and "helping" is enormous.

For Greg to have been helpful, Liz needed to ask questions with possible solutions. The vaguer her questions, the more she would become a damsel in distress—and the more Greg would feel the need to be a knight in shining armor.

Alternative #2

Liz might have asked Greg to help her, without falling into the trap of asking him to save her, in a different way. It is possible, of course, that she simply couldn't come up with any possible solutions on her own. She might have been too frightened by her thoughts to think productively.

In that case she could have approached Greg quite honestly by saying something like this:

"I'm feeling very unhappy and frightened and I'm not even sure whether I have any real reason to be feeling this way. I've got thoughts flying around in my head and need to get them all out. Do you think you could just listen and be a sounding board for me? Maybe if I just verbalize it all I'll be able to get some kind of handle on what it is that's bugging me."

There's nothing wrong with letting it all hang out, as long as you've made it clear that that's what you're doing . . . as long as you're not expecting your lover/husband to do the work of putting it all together. The "sounding board" request doesn't put pressure on the sounding board. A man who wants to be helpful—like Greg—will be able to make himself listen better when he doesn't feel obligated to come up with *the* solution.

Unless women want to be married to men who attempt to control their lives, they cannot expect their husbands to be anything but good consultants. As soon as women ask for more, they are, in effect, saying, "Please. Take over and manage my life. Tell me exactly what to do, when to do it, and how to do it." And when women ask that of the men in their lives they have to expect intervention of that nature in every sphere of their relationship. They can't just pick and choose.

Men's Fear of Femininity

Men tend to resist identifying with women's AVBs for two reasons. First, as we said earlier, people in a position of power don't like to see themselves in a position of powerlessness. And second, we live in a particularly homophobic culture.

Rita S. was thirty-eight when she fell in love with Peter, a man she met at work. They are both architects at a large firm. Shortly after they became involved they found an apartment together, and a year later they married.

"I was absolutely head-over-heels in love with Peter," Rita recalls. "I mean, all of that stuff about bells ringing and waves crashing to the shore . . . it was all true. And I still feel that way."

They've been married for five years and had a child three years ago.

"It's funny," Rita says, "but I remember talking to girl-friends about Peter shortly after we met and telling them that he was just like a woman. That talking to him was like talking to one of my women friends." Rita laughs. "I was once having that conversation with a friend on the phone and Peter overheard it. He was terribly upset. When I hung up he told me that he'd heard me say that to several of my friends and that he really didn't like it.

"I tried to explain what I meant. I really meant it as a compliment. I meant that he was sensitive, and loving, and affectionate, and gentle, and that he talked about things from the perspective of feelings. Most of my girlfriends can't talk to their husbands the way I talk to Peter. They have no idea what their wives are talking about. But Peter did . . . and does. And until I'd met him I'd never known a man I could talk to that way.

"Well, Peter was mollified by my explanation. But he told me that he wasn't all that 'gentle' and 'sweet.' And that even if he was, he didn't like being described as 'womanlike.' So I made jokes about how tough he was. But I never really pushed it and I didn't talk about him that way to friends when he was around. My friends knew what I meant. They didn't think I was casting any aspersions on his manhood. But I really felt that he was bothered by it."

Rita understands intuitively that "femininity" is a valuable quality in a man. Dr. John K. Antill, a psychologist at Australia's Macquarie University, came to the same conclusion after studying more than one hundred marriages. His findings were recently reported in *The Journal of Personality and Social Psychology:* "The results provide substantial evidence for the importance of femininity in relationships; the happiness of the husband was positively related to the wife's femininity, and the happiness of the wife was positively related to the husband's femininity." In other words, Dr. Antill found that the happiest marriages were those in which both partners were more feminine.

When Dr. Antill talks about femininity he is talking about the same kinds of traits we discussed in Chapter 2; which are the same kinds of traits Rita was thinking of when she described Peter to her friends. It makes a great deal of sense, in the context of all we've discussed so far, that femininity would be a valuable quality in a relationship.

All of the women and men we've discussed in this chapter are attempting to forge new identities for themselves. They have a sense of what it is they want in life, and they are looking for ways to get it. In past generations the answers had been laid out. Young women and young men looked to their parents and grandparents to determine what they could "want" and to determine how they could get it as well. As we said earlier, the goals of both men and women are changing. And the life-style that was built around the attainment of those old goals is no longer comfortable.

Clearly, women and men cannot simply turn their backs on a life-style they spent the better part of their childhoods absorbing. Rather, in the process of forging new identities men and women need to examine their childhood AVBs and examine each other's childhood AVBs as well. Essentially, they need to retain those things that can be of value and learn to use them properly. Women, after all, have received a lifetime of training in the realm of relationships. Characteristics like openness, a willingness to make oneself vulnerable, a willingness to acknowledge feelings and emotions are all, as we'll see, critical to the success of a relationship.

It would, indeed, be tragic if career women lost sight of the value of these qualities or abandoned them for masculine AVBs instead of sharing them with the men in their lives.

As men and women begin to develop new definitions of "masculine" and "feminine," they will be better equipped to see each other realistically . . . to have realistic expectations of each other and of their relationships. Which brings us to Part III.

Part III

THE OBJECTS
OF OUR AFFECTIONS

CHAPTER 6

Who Is the Perfect Man?

Looking for Unicorns

We asked the women we interviewed to tell us about whom they saw as the "perfect man." It wasn't a trick question. Clearly, most women recognize that this "perfect man" will probably never materialize. "What's the point?" a number of them asked. "It's too frustrating to talk about." "Look," said Eleanor J., a chemist at a very large food-processing corporation, "I happen to be a very talented woman. I'm not being immodest when I say that. It's the truth. I can sit in my laboratory and create all sorts of things. But I haven't yet managed to figure out a way to create the perfect man for myself. So why bother talking about it."

In fact, there are several compelling reasons for women to talk about what they think of when they imagine the "perfect man." Regardless of whether or not they believe they will ever meet this man—regardless of what they have reconciled themselves to as "reality"—when women talk about "the perfect man," they are expressing who it is they *long for.* And it's important to acknowledge longings. Those longings say something about values that are operating under the surface.

When the women we interviewed allowed themselves to let go of their inhibitions and really talk about their "ideal man" they became excited. And many of them felt embarrassed when they heard their own excitement. They wanted too much. They wanted more than they were allowed. When they thought about their yearnings they felt needy and vulnerable, so they called upon "logic-think" to tuck the desires away—nice and tidy—where they wouldn't interfere with the business of life. Career women could not afford to go into the work world burdened by vulnerability.

The problem is that wishing those desires away does not make them vanish. The notion that if we don't talk about longings we won't feel them is simply not true. Desires are no less frustrating when pushed into our unconscious. They simply exist buried—an unidentifiable source of frustration. When people deny their longings they feel as if they're being tickled by an invisible feather. They can't see it, so they can't grab hold of it; and eventually, their frustration turns into anger or depression. The point of acknowledging longings is to make the feather visible, and begin to figure out a way of effectively dealing with our wishes.

The fact that Eleanor recognizes intellectually that she can't go into her laboratory and concoct a perfect man for herself doesn't mean that she doesn't try, unconsciously, to re-create the men she does meet; to make them into something that they are not.

"I think that the perfect man is like a unicorn," Lydia K., a theater critic, says. "He's only visible to virgins . . . to women who have never been in a real relationship. Once you lose your virginity and attempt to get something going with a real, flesh-and-blood man, the perfect man disappears from sight. He becomes mythological." She pauses before she adds, "But from time to time I still find myself looking for unicorns."

In this chapter we will examine what it is that successful women *wish for* in a man, and then try to understand how much of a hold that wish has on them.

The New Macho

"The perfect man!" says Beth, a physical therapist who recently set up a private practice with two orthopedists. "I'm too old to believe in fairy tales . . . and too jaded," she adds, "but I'll give it a whirl. I guess if I could have everything I wanted in a man I'd want him to be very smart . . . that's really important to me. I hate the idea of being with a guy who isn't as smart as I am. And I'd want him to have a very strong sense of himself . . . to be very strong emotionally. I have a very hard time with passive, wishy-washy guys. Also, I'd want him to really love his work, and to be good at it. No," Beth reconsiders, "I'd want him to be brilliant at it . . . a real star. Dynamic. World renowned," she adds, laughing. Then, with mock seriousness, "Do you think that's too much to ask?"

Allison F., a forty-year-old obstetrician, said, "My idea of a perfect man is someone who is sophisticated enough to handle himself in any situation. He wouldn't have to look like Cary Grant—although I wouldn't mind—but he'd have to have that kind of savoir faire. And I guess another part of that would involve a sense of humor. I really would place a lot of importance on his having a sense of humor."

"The most important thing to me in a man is that he have good character," said Vera K., who's recently ended a fifteen-year marriage. What does she mean by good character? "Well, I guess the usual sort of thing," she explained. "A very clear sense of himself. Someone who really knows what he wants and goes after it. Aggressive. Someone I could rely on.

That's what I think of as good character in a man. Someone who's reliable and serious and really strong emotionally. Someone who's really there for me whenever I need him."

Other women were more specific than the three we just described. One said, "My ideal man would have read all of Proust . . . in French." Another said, "He'd be very worldly. Really well traveled. And he'd be fluent in about six languages. And he'd write poems to me in each one. And he'd be tall. I'm a pretty big woman and I need to be with a guy who's bigger than I am." Another said, "He'd be a perfect blend of fun and seriousness; responsible and carefree; gorgeous, but not vain. Well, I take back the gorgeous. Just good-looking and well dressed." Then she paused and asked, "Do all of the women you talk to say the same thing?"

Indeed, most of the women talked about the same things when they summoned up their images of perfect men. They didn't all care about Proust, but they did all care about appearance (translation: presentability, sophistication, etc.); reliability (translation: "being there," strong, take-charge); and productivity (translation: achievement and success).

If those qualities have a familiar ring, it's because they come directly from the childhood AVBs we discussed in Chapter 2. The fantasy man these women long for is an update of the "good husband" they learned, as children, to pursue. "Dynamic," "aggressive," and "together" are, in essence, new euphemisms for *macho.*

It's important to also note the fact that each of those criteria for a "perfect man"—appearance, reliability, and productivity—involves externals, or tangibles. None of them touches on intangibles like feelings.

One woman, Elizabeth F., a thirty-six-year-old doctor, went through a list of qualities very much like the ones above. "He'd be bright, and attractive, and successful," she explained enthusiastically. Then, as an afterthought she said, "And, of course, he'd have to have all the cliché traits also: sweet, tender, trustworthy. Things like that."

Elizabeth was one of a handful of women who even mentioned qualities that were rooted in emotions—traditional
feminine qualities—when she was asked about the perfect
man. And her mention of those qualities was, significantly,
prefaced by a disclaimer. She labeled them "cliché." There's
nothing cliché about such traits as sweetness, tenderness, and
trustworthiness in the context of an intimate relationship.
Indeed, based on Dr. Antill's findings, the capacity to em-
body those traditionally "feminine" traits is critical to the
success of a relationship.

Yet Elizabeth feels the need to apologize for mentioning
her desire for a "sweet, tender, trustworthy" man. As a child
she learned to think of those qualities as being "feminine."
And the male AVBs of the work world Elizabeth chose to
enter as an adult equated "feminine" with "frivolous." Her
acceptance of that equation is causing her problems.

The Problem with Those Standards

The three external standards most of the women used
when they described their image of the perfect man—appearance, reliability, and productivity—are the same standards people use in the workplace when hiring. And they're
the same standards specialists use in mergers and acquisi-
tions when they try to determine whether or not a corporation would make a good acquisition. Will it enhance our
corporate image? Do they have a solid, reliable foundation?
Does their bottom line project productivity and profit?

These are good questions in the right place. Years ago, it
was appropriate for women to ask those questions of the men
with whom they planned "mergers" because, as we said earlier, years ago it was the "work" of women—in the most
pragmatic sense—to acquire "good" husbands. Women relied on their husbands to project good images for them, to be
consistent, and to produce a healthy profit. Today, however,

women can produce their own profit. They are capable of projecting an image of their own making, independent of the men in their lives. They have developed their own resources, both emotional and financial.

What then, do they need from men? Indeed, that's the question today's achieving women need to ask. In the process of answering it they will be forced to reconsider what it is they should be looking for when they look for men. Eventually they will develop new criteria for evaluating men—criteria that mesh with their needs.

Developing New Standards Vs. Lowering Old Ones

When we talk to achievement-oriented women about reexamining their criteria for judging men, many of them react defensively. "I suppose you're telling me that I have to be willing to settle," one woman said when the issue of standards came up. She was angry. She had worked hard to be "the best." Why should she have to accept anything less than "the best" when it came to a life-partner? "It's very difficult for me to accept mediocrity," she said firmly. "I just don't feel like settling. But I don't feel like being alone either. It drives me crazy to think that the only way I can avoid being alone is to settle."

Her sentiments were echoed in interview after interview. If one could have the best, why settle for second best? Settling for second best is like accepting failure, and for successful women in particular, the feeling of having failed is very uncomfortable. They are accustomed to achieving what they set out to achieve.

Unfortunately, they are so caught up in their pursuit of excellence that they have difficulty stepping back to reevaluate whether or not what they are pursuing as "best" is, in fact, best for them. When they establish that distance they invariably discover that the answer to their search doesn't rest on their willingness to *lower* their old standards. It rests, rather, on their willingness to examine their criteria for judging men. Do these criteria enable them to detect the kind of man who can meet their needs? If not, they need to find more suitable criteria. These women, once they develop new standards, will not be seeking "less than the best." They will simply be seeking something different.

Pursuing the Intangible

The new criteria we will discuss address intangible—emotional—needs. Women, regardless of what they do for a living, are clearly more than the sum of their accomplishments. Much like men, they are the sum of their feelings as well. Essentially, today's career women need men for precisely the same reason men need women. They both need a safe, nurturing place in which their feelings can be accepted . . . and thereby validated. "What do I *need* a man for?" women need to ask. "Because I need to hold someone and have someone hold me," they will answer. "I need to express my tenderness and I need to be treated tenderly." "I need the ongoing constancy of one person to whom I can trust my feelings, and I need to hear the evolution of his feelings over the course of time."

When women begin to believe that they can acknowledge those "feminine" needs without risking their career success, they will begin to replace their old criteria for success with new ones without worrying about losing face. Indeed, they will be able to pursue new criteria with their uniquely feminine energy.

Recognizing a "Satisfying" Relationship

"Success" is a word that belongs more in the world of work than the world of a relationship. It relates to such tangibles as productivity and achievement. Its opposite is "failure."

The ideas of success and failure have more to do with conquering the outside world than with relationships. Women are not *hunting* for men. They are seeking to expand their emotional satisfactions. When they look outside, they become primarily dependent upon external criteria for fulfillment. And women by now should have learned from history that when they are dependent solely on externals as to what would best fulfill their needs they end up being disappointed.

When they turn to their own resources and look at their own feelings they are more likely to find values they can trust and believe in. When you begin to judge a relationship on issues like "satisfaction" and "emotional fulfillment," rather than on success, you ask yourself all sorts of valuable questions. "How do I feel when I'm with him?" a woman might ask herself. "Do I feel as if I'm accepted/appreciated/valued?" "Do I feel as if I can be myself?" "Do I feel as if he can be himself when he's with me?" "Do I value/appreciate/accept him?"

Indeed, when a woman stops worrying about "success" and begins to focus on "contentment," she finds herself less concerned with what other people think about the man in her life. Other people cannot know how she feels, inside, when she is alone with a man (or simply alone), and so they are in no position to make judgments.

"I've got a group of friends," said Theresa M., an account executive with a large advertising agency, "who are very quick-witted. They're mostly from the business. When we get together there's lots of quick repartee. It's a little overwhelming at first. In fact, I think there's a competitive edge to it. I love it. It's something that I'm very good at. But when Jerry—my boyfriend—first joined the group for an evening he had an awful time. He really hated the whole thing. He's a chemist. He's very serious and basically just isn't accustomed to the kind of banter that goes on with my friends. After that first evening I think he may have felt inadequate. Actually, I think I experienced him as being inadequate.

"When we left the dinner party to go home, he suggested that we go listen to some music together first. I was surprised because it was very late, and Jerry's usually pretty eager to get home. We went to a nice piano bar, ordered some more wine, and listened to Marian McPartland. It was very soothing. After a while Jerry said that he wanted to go home with me because he needed to be alone with me in the kind of place *he feels comfortable.* He said it was like rinsing a bad taste out of his mouth.

"For a moment, after he said that, I felt defensive. But then I thought how nice it was that he wanted to be alone with me. We went home and made love. And the next morning we went out for the Sunday paper and spent the day going through it. I just feel so *at home* with Jerry. It's hard, really, to explain.

"Well, Monday, at the office, some people made jokes about my *mad scientist.* To tell you the truth, I couldn't have cared less. Most of them went home alone that night. I wouldn't have traded my weekend with any of them. And if they were in a position to feel what I feel when I'm with Jerry, I think they'd probably understand. It really is a relief."

The feeling of relief comes from not having to strive for success. Theresa travels in a fast-paced, high-powered world where she is always under pressure to perform. Additional pressure of that sort is the last thing she needs in her personal relationships. When she thinks about marrying Jerry she worries some about whether or not she'd have to give up her friends but decides that she won't.

"Jerry is pretty reasonable. I think he'd agree to see them from time to time. And I know that he could care less about my seeing them without him, which is probably what I'll do. I don't need him to be on my arm whenever I step out. I think things will fall into place." Most likely, they will.

A Closer Look at "The Perfect Couple"

The *appearance* of a good relationship and the *reality* of a good relationship are, as skyrocketing divorce rates have taught us, two very separate issues. Outsiders make judgments about whether or not a relationship is successful based on the external standards we have just discussed. But those standards don't necessarily reflect the experience of the people involved in the relationship. They don't reflect whether or not the people involved find solace and tenderness in each other.

"My first marriage was perfect," said Edith F., a woman who began a career in merchandising after twenty years of being a wife and homemaker. "My husband was handsome, smart, and a pillar of the community. He was a surgeon. We met in college and got married before he started medical school. Everyone was thrilled. We were Dr. and Mrs. Perfect.

"The only problem with the relationship," Edith continued, "was that we were totally and utterly isolated from each other. I don't think he was really a bad person. I just think he was busy being the all-American success story. And in the process, I was left home alone. Even when I was with him I was alone. He never took the trouble to notice anything I was feeling. And I never had the courage to tell him. Who was I to feel anything but ecstatic? I had everything I could have wanted.

"I think at least two dozen people must have fallen off their feet when they heard about our separation. And I'm sure that many more than that thought I was out of my mind. All I knew was that if I didn't get out of that picture I would have *really* gone out of my mind. I need to be touched and recognized in a relationship. I don't think that's too much to ask. When I look at men now, that's what I look for."

When Edith first met her husband she saw him, quite clearly, through the eyes of her childhood AVBs. And her perception was 20/20. He *was* a good catch by those standards. The problem is that those standards had absolutely nothing to do with Edith's need for intimate companionship. Her need for that sort of companionship simply went unmet —until she could no longer bear her isolation. Her pain forced her to reevaluate her standards.

Looking for Trust and Goodwill

The most critical issues a financially independent woman needs to consider when she looks for a man with whom she will be intimately involved is whether or not that man can be trusted with her innermost feelings—as opposed to the facade she presents in the workplace; and whether or not she is willing to be tender and caring with his innermost feelings —as opposed to demanding that he be the same with her as he is in his workplace.

Good intentions may not count for much in the work world. They even say that the "road to hell is paved" with them. But good intentions—the fact that you wish well for your partner—coupled with the kind of *trust* we have just described, are critical in an intimate relationship.

"I'm convinced that the way I got through my marriage is because I honestly believed that Joe always had goodwill; that he was committed to making our relationship work and that he had the best of intentions," said Bonnie J., who has been married to the same man for thirty years. "There were times when I felt bruised. Incredibly painful times for both of us. But on some level I always trusted that Joe was not vicious. He wishes our family well. I honestly believe that about him, and because I believe that I can get past the heat of an argument.

"Afterwards, when we've both cooled down, we can figure out what it was about. He forces himself to look at himself honestly, and I do the same. Actually, we do it for 'us,' really, and that brings us back to the fact that we have something very precious. We can look at what happened and try to understand it. That's where the "good intentions" come in. I trust that Joe will always try—at least try—to look at what he's done if I tell him that he's hurt me. That's all I can ask for."

Throughout this chapter we have been discussing what it is that women look for when they look for men. Who are the men that career women think of as "perfect"? Most of the women with whom we spoke continue to imagine the "perfect man" as he was laid out for them during childhood. The focus of those childhood AVBs is, as we've said throughout, on externals—looks, productivity, accomplishment. Relationships based solely on these old standards inevitably leave both partners feeling isolated.

Achieving women need to develop new standards by which to judge men—standards that focus more on emotional availability than productivity, more on trustworthiness than on appearance, and more on goodwill than on accomplishment. In order to do that, these women must first say farewell to fantasy and begin to accept reality—even if it doesn't always meet the high standards they set for themselves. We'll delve into that reality in Chapter 7.

CHAPTER 7

Farewell Fantasy, Hello Reality

Looking for Real People

We talked, in Chapter 6, about the ways in which women continue to cling to the fantasy of a perfect man. Indeed, for many such women the idea of letting go of that fantasy is frightening. Intellectually, they understand that they need to develop more reality-based expectations of men and of relationships. Emotionally, however, they are frightened. They wonder *how* one goes about abandoning a fantasy that goes back as long as they can remember. And they are frightened about what they will get to replace that fantasy.

Indeed, when ambitious, achieving women stop looking for the perfect man and begin looking for another person with whom to share their lives—another person with strengths and vulnerabilities—they will have integrated both autonomy and intimacy and be able to enjoy the security that comes from that experience. Before they can get to that point, however, they have to develop new standards for judging themselves and men. These standards, as we said earlier, are based more on feelings than on accomplishments.

Shifting standards from exterior (i.e., appearance, reliability, productivity) to interior (i.e., fulfillment, real feelings, trust/good intentions) is not, by any means, an easy process . . . particularly for career women. Career women learned to reject a set of childhood AVBs that emphasized feelings and relationships, and they were positively rewarded in the work world for their ability to focus on product and the bottom line. We are not suggesting, however, that when women return to the realm of feelings, they return also to a position of dependency. We are not suggesting that they abandon their achievement for the realm of emotions. Quite the contrary. We are suggesting that they begin to believe in their own accomplishment as a permanent piece of their identity, and that they enrich their lives by addressing their emotional needs as well.

Focusing on Accomplishment

Many women who went on to have successful professional lives grew up in families that emphasized and rewarded accomplishment, often to the neglect of any accompanying feelings. Dory, for example, got her MBA from Harvard a few years ago and is a bond trader on Wall Street. Her life's passion is theater. "As a kid," she recalled, "I used to love to put on shows. I'd get everyone in the neighborhood together and write a script and do set design and direct . . . the works. The effort would culminate in a huge extravaganza in our living room. I remember once overhearing my mother— who was very proud of everything I did—telling a neighbor that I had masterminded the entire show. 'She can do anything,' my mother boasted. 'She's got a talent for pulling things together. She's a real self-starter. Someday she'll be president of a big company.' "

Dory's mother was right. She did have a remarkable talent for organization. Women like Dory can thank their parents for recognizing and encouraging their accomplishments. That recognition contributed to their success. Their parents got pleasure from their accomplishments—i.e., the ability to put on shows, or to get good grades, or to be an athlete—and their pleasure became their children's reward. Children have an enormous investment in making their parents happy.

The problem is that Dory's parents didn't address the pleasure Dory experienced when she organized one of her shows. They weren't sensitive to the emotional meaning of this "show biz" activity for her. As a result, Dory learned that her sense of self had more to do with achievement than with the feelings she experienced while she was doing what she loved. Dory came to view accomplishment as the *sine qua non* of a person, and today she applies the same yardstick in her appraisal of men. In truth, Dory—and many of the men she considers inappropriate—have much more depth and texture than a listing of their accomplishments would indicate.

We asked Dory what she wanted in a man. "Well," she said, sounding like many of the women we talked to, "I want a man who's bright and good at what he does. A man who sets high standards for himself the way I do for myself. And," she added, "I'd have to find a man who loves theater the way I do. Even though I'm not involved with theater professionally, it's really a part of me."

We asked Dory why, given that theater was really a part of her, she felt that any man with whom she became involved had to like theater too. After all, we reasoned, why couldn't she go to the theater with friends who share her enthusiasm, and come home to a man who is passionate about other things? For sure, it's very *nice* for a woman who likes theater to be involved with a man who likes going to the theater; but there's a significant difference between seeing it as a nice quality in a man and believing that it's a prerequisite for being involved with him.

Dory was shocked by our suggestion. "I just . . . I just," she stammered uncharacteristically, "I just don't think I'd find anyone who wasn't interested in theater very interesting." Albert Schweitzer? "Well," she countered, "let's not be absurd. The point is that I don't think someone could understand *me* without really knowing and loving theater."

Until recently Dory had been dating a man she met through work. "He was a nice guy. Very bright. But he's a perfect example of what happens when I date a guy who doesn't like theater. Ted never went to the theater. He was a film freak and said he had no patience for the stage. For my birthday, he bought me two tickets to *Nicholas Nickelby* and wrote a note about how of all the people he knew, I was one who deserved to see this show. The extra ticket was because he knows I don't like to go to the theater alone. He said I should take one of my theater-loving friends. I mean," Dory said incredulously, "he didn't even want to come with me to see the major theatrical event of the decade."

Dory missed the significance of Ted's gift, and in so doing, she missed the fact that Ted met certain critical criteria that qualified him very well for an intimate relationship. When Ted bought the *Nickelby* ticket for Dory he was telling her that despite the fact that he felt differently, he understood and appreciated *her* feelings about theater. That focus of feelings—which Dory learned to tune out as a child—is much more critical to her future happiness than a focus on theater.

Focusing on Appearances

Sharon S., a biologist who has never been in a long-term relationship told us about a man she was involved with last summer, and the circumstances that led her to break off the relationship. "I spent some time this summer with someone who I liked quite a lot. He was really a nice, sweet guy. A lot of fun to be with.

"I'm thirty-two years old and I really want to have a husband and children in my life. I went to the beach this summer having made a definite decision to be less picky about guys than I had been because I feel like my life is zipping by and I'm scared of missing out on the things that I care most about. So, when I first got involved with Thomas I made myself withhold judgments and try to just have a good time.

"But after a few weeks out at the beach—we each took our vacation there at the same time—it became hard not to notice some things. For example, Thomas is just not at all verbal. He has tremendous difficulty verbalizing his feelings and thoughts. It's not that he's at all stupid. In fact, he's very bright. He's just more visual than verbal. He takes spectacular photographs. But I love to have conversations with people, and Thomas is a real listener.

"Still, I found him fun to be with . . . easy and pleasant. He's a very warm kind of person, and I appreciate that. So I tried not to think about the fact that he didn't talk as much as I do. Little by little, though, I began to think that maybe one reason he didn't talk much was because he didn't have all that much to say. I mean, he hadn't read any of the books I asked him about. He always had a mystery in his back pocket and I began to wonder if maybe that was all he read. And I don't think he had ever been in therapy, which is very important to me. I felt like he just didn't have the same kind of language as I . . . he didn't share my experience.

"But I didn't want to be too hasty because the fact was that for some reason I really enjoyed my time with him. I found myself looking forward to seeing him, and he always seemed so happy to be with me. He was easy to have fun with.

"We got together with some friends one night and I was sort of watching him closely. It was then that I realized that the gap was too big . . . that I didn't feel all that good about him. People were talking about film, and he had nothing to contribute to the conversation. He just sat there all evening. I kept waiting for him to say something, but he didn't. When we left, he told me that he'd really had a good time. I couldn't believe him, but he really seemed to be in a very good mood.

"Well," Sharon continued, "little by little I started feeling pretty turned off by him. To this day I think he's a very sweet man, but I could never imagine marrying him. He's just not very dynamic. In fact, the thought of being married to him makes me feel very anxious. As Thomas got more and more serious, I got more and more anxious. I stopped having fun. In fact, it got to the point, by the end of the summer, that I'd get sick when we were supposed to get together. I wasn't faking it either. I'd get terrible headaches, or nausea. Something real . . . but the coincidence was too strong.

"Finally, I just told him that I didn't think it was going to work and that I didn't want to see him anymore. I think he was really hurt, and I felt bad about it. But it wasn't worth the anxiety I was going through. Sometimes now I wonder if I made a mistake. I mean, I'm still alone and there's no one special on the horizon. And he really was a sweet guy. But I figure I'll just hang in there for a while longer and try not to panic."

Sharon was able to enjoy Thomas a great deal until she began to think about him "seriously." Then she stopped having fun. That's when she began to start comparing him to her fantasies . . . fantasies that continue to shape her standards. Thomas clearly wasn't Sharon's idea of a "perfect man," and despite her effort to ease up on her standards she discovered that there were certain areas in which she was unable to bend. Thomas simply was not "presentable."

Sharon's concern about Thomas's presentability harks back to the days when women took their identities from men. Sharon is worried about her identity. She thought about the way Thomas presented himself at the party and asked herself, "Do I want to be seen this way?" When she answered her own question with a "No," the only possible solution seemed to be to dispose of Thomas. She wasn't able to distance her own self, her own identity from his—despite the fact that she had thoroughly enjoyed her time with him—in order to say, "People see Thomas one way and me another. They may not understand why we're together, but I know how good I feel when I'm with him."

As soon as Sharon began to place great importance on Thomas's appearance, the issue of how she felt when they were together took a backseat. Performance took priority over feelings. In fact, after a while those feelings got pushed so far back that Sharon lost them. The reality of what they had enjoyed together for most of the summer became secondary to the kind of standards Sharon used when she talked about a "perfect man." Although Sharon is quick to talk of her willingness to "compromise," she still hasn't deviated from the substance of those early AVBs to relax and find someone who makes her feel good.

The idea of marrying a man who didn't project the image of intelligence that Sharon was concerned with projecting made Sharon anxious. Since Sharon is perfectly capable of projecting this image on her own—and does so—we must stop and ask ourselves why it is so important to her that the man in her life project the same image. Indeed, she cares so much about Thomas's less-than-vibrant image that she becomes sick over it. Sharon's independence—and her ability to project herself as an individual—feels good, but it doesn't feel very real. She wants a man who will confirm it for the rest of the world, and in the process, confirm it for her.

Sharon feels fine about who she is when she's not involved with a man because as long as she's single she can hold on to her fantasy of the perfect man. She can think about possibly meeting him and what a lovely life they'd make together for everyone to see. Such a man, she reasons, wouldn't take anything away from her. She'd still be the woman she worked hard to be and she'd have him as well. Indeed, having such a man would offer her a kind of insurance. If, for any reason, her career suddenly nose-dived, or if she chose to stop working, she'd still be safe. The perfect man would be able to take care of her—and of her image—regardless of how her fortunes turned. Being involved with such a man is like walking the high wire with a net.

What about a less-than-perfect man? As soon as Sharon got involved with a man who couldn't reinforce her own image, she felt vulnerable. And she got sick. Once you marry a man like Thomas you really are independent in many ways. And so is he. Thomas might have had a dandy time at the party. He might have found another mystery buff. He might have enjoyed just eating and watching people. But Sharon didn't allow either herself or Thomas the room for either of them to explore those possibilities. She was too concerned about what he was projecting to her friends and how that projection would reflect on her.

She wasn't being meanspirited. She was, in fact, very fond of Thomas. But she was frightened. If she ended up marrying a man like him, she would have to let go of the fantasy of finding the man she dreamed about when she was a little girl. And as soon as she let go of that, her independence became chillingly real. For Sharon, it became more real than she was prepared to accept. It was easier to focus on whether or not Thomas met her standards . . . regardless of where those standards brought her.

Helaine and Adam: Good Man/Bad Husband

Holding on to an obsolete image of the perfect man is also a way of avoiding the kind of vulnerability that comes with genuine intimacy. We'll talk more about people's fears of intimacy in Chapter 8. For now, it's enough to understand that as women begin to let go of their fantasy-mates and replace them with real people, they will begin to feel more vulnerable. Sharon, for example, felt terribly vulnerable when she thought about marrying Thomas. Those feelings of vulnerability are neither bad nor good. They are simply there and they need to be experienced.

To be sure, the feelings are painful and frightening. But they can't kill you. In fact, it's probably more dangerous to spend the rest of your life avoiding these feelings than it is simply to experience them.

One woman, Helaine P., a radiologist, described a particularly touching incident with a man she found herself caring deeply for.

"I started dating Adam in 1969," she began. "We'd both been out of college for a year and those were, as you probably remember, very turbulent times. I lived and worked in New York, and he lived and worked about half an hour south of Philadelphia. So he used to come in every weekend and stay with me.

"He really was a terrific guy. He was one of the first men I really enjoyed sleeping with. And he was very bright. And incredibly intuitive. I think I was in love with him. And it scared me to death. The thing about Adam was that he was really committed to his political ideals. I mean, I was political because the air you breathed in those days was political. And I'm still involved in politics to some degree. But I'm basically the same sort of liberal that my parents were.

"Adam, on the other hand, really wanted to make a life out of his politics. He worked as a sort of social worker in a working-class area, and he was always running off to this meeting and that rally. I admired it, but I didn't want it to be my life. And for some reason back then—maybe because I was so young—I assumed that if it was his life it would also be mine."

One of the reasons Helaine assumed that her husband would determine her life-style and politics was that she grew up believing that he would have the power to do so. But she expected to meet a man who could do that without creating any personal conflict for her. She didn't. She met and fell in love with Adam, and she realized that if she decided to marry him she would have to pursue her own career and work out a mutually agreeable life-style with him—a prospect that seemed impossible to her.

"Little by little I began creating distance between us. I actually played a trick on myself. I started feeling like I didn't care for him. I began finding all sorts of things about him annoying. I picked stupid fights with him. Finally, one Saturday night we went out to a movie and came home to go to bed. We made love, and it was all right, and then Adam started talking about the movie we'd just seen in a very critical way. Well, I loved the movie, and our discussion turned into a huge fight. It was a little after midnight and I asked him to leave. I knew that there were buses back to Philly every hour and I just didn't want to have him around.

"He got dressed, packed up his little bag, and left. The next day he called me early and said, 'Helaine, I really care for you and I'm not going to let you push me away like this.'" Helaine's eyes filled with tears. "It's so ridiculous," she said. "This happened ten years ago. We saw each other for a while after that but I was too formidable for him. I was a better pusher than he was a guard. And anyway, after a while he probably got tired of investing so much energy in keeping me close." Helaine paused for a long sigh. "The thing is that I was overwhelmed by how tender he was. That he even noticed that I was pushing him away. He didn't just get angry at me for sending him on a two-hour bus trip in the middle of the night. He cared enough to figure out what I was doing. And it scared me to death."

Helaine pushed Adam away just as she was beginning to appreciate having him close because she didn't think she'd be able to have the kind of life with him that she'd have if she married the "perfect man"—that man she learned to look for when she was a child. On an intellectual level Helaine is troubled by her rejection of so "tender" a man. On an emotional level, she finds him unacceptable. Sharon explained it very well. She said, quite simply, that she began to get anxious whenever she thought about marrying Thomas.

Helaine and Sharon, and other successful, achieving women like them, believe that the perfect man—the unicorn they are struggling not only to see, but to hold—will give them things. If he is successful, he will give them the feeling of being successful, as well as the accoutrements of success. "Look," Helaine said quite bluntly, "is it so wrong to want a nice life for myself? I'm not enormously materialistic, but I like having nice clothing. I'd like to have a nice home. I'd like to have kids and be able to give them things the way my parents gave me things."

There is nothing wrong with *wishing* to have all of the things Helaine just described. In fact, there's nothing wrong with *wishing* a man would give them to you. It's a problem, however, when a woman's pursuit of the ideal man causes her to lose touch with the reality of her own resources. Helaine, for example, doesn't *need* a man to buy her a nice house. She's a successful woman. She can afford to buy one on her own. Yet Helaine sabotaged a relationship with a real, live man whom she liked because he couldn't give her those things by himself. On some level she seems to believe that a man who cannot give her the things she wants will take away her ability to give them to herself.

If Helaine continues to look—either consciously or unconsciously—for men to meet her childhood AVBs she may eventually find one. But such a man may be as tied to his childhood system as she is to hers. He too may want a relationship focusing on things, rather than feelings. And he would then expect the appropriate deference in return. Indeed, such a man is more likely than Adam to take away the things Helaine values.

Kate and George—Weighing the Priorities

Kate was—essentially—forced by her lover to examine her priorities and make a commitment. She had been seeing George exclusively for two years when he began to press for marriage. Her reaction to the pressure was, at first, utter panic. And when the panic subsided she was faced with what felt like a difficult situation.

"I guess I just assumed that we'd go on this way forever," Kate commented. "I never really thought I'd get married. I'm not interested in having children, and George has grown children from an early marriage. When marriage suddenly became important to George it terrified me. I mean, I love George, I suppose, and I don't really have any interest in dating other men, but things about him just don't measure up to this idea that I have about 'the man I would marry.'

"Marriage," Kate said with a long sigh. "My God. Whenever I think about marrying George, all I can think of is a long list of weak points. A few months ago, for example, we were at a big party and I looked across the room and saw George standing and talking to someone and he was laughing too loudly. You could hear him across the room. All I could think of was that he appeared to me to be an absolute schmuck, and I felt like anyone looking at him would see him that way. How could I possibly marry him if I look at him across a crowded room and think he looks like an absolute schmuck?"

Kate had an image. The man she wanted to marry was supposed to appear some enchanted evening, like a prince, across a crowded room. It didn't even occur to her that some other person at the party might have seen George with a different, and more interested eye. Some women across the room, for example, might have been captivated by his energy. But, even more important, Kate didn't recognize that her insistence that George never look like a schmuck was as much a burden on her as it was on him.

As long as women seek to mate with ideals rather than real people, they are denying themselves the chance to fulfill their need to be real people in real relationships. The more pressured your work life is, the more you need your homelife to be a place where you can let go. And "letting go" means relaxing your stringent standards—for yourself as well as him —and still being loved. Women who dress to the teeth for work every day might need to hang out in their pajamas all day Saturday. If such a woman lives with a man who always needs to see her looking as though she just stepped out of a bandbox, she won't have the freedom to let go of her work image.

It's helpful to think of an intimate relationship as though it were an environment. Indeed, an intimate relationship is an emotional environment, and when it's healthy, it's an environment in which neither partner needs to think about being at the head of the class. Such concerns are, simply, inappropriate to the environment.

George, who is an oncologist, spends much of his workday keeping his emotional responses in check. At a party, he laughs too loud. He laughs louder than Kate is comfortable with. Would she be happier with George if he carried his restraints from his professional life into his private life? Clearly not. His willingness over the years to be there emotionally for Kate is the direct result of his ability to drop his work facade when he's with her . . . an ability that is often difficult for doctors who frequently confuse intimacy with "bedside manner."

Before George began pushing the issue of marriage, Kate didn't have to worry about how he reflected on her. Suddenly, she can think of little else. "I keep weighing things in my head," she explained. What does laughing too loud at a party have to do with George's ability to be a loving husband? Kate is worried for good reason. She doesn't want to lose the intimacy she's enjoyed with George over the last two years.

If women are honest when they express their desire for intimate relationships, then why do they put up roadblocks? When they stop searching for ideals—for the men they have a "right" to—they will begin to see whole people. To be sure, for all the reasons we've discussed, women will be reluctant to lay aside their search for the perfect man. And men will be reluctant to lay aside their search for the perfect woman. In the process of helping each other, however, they will be moving toward intimacy.

George helped Kate by setting forth what amounted to an ultimatum. "He told me that it was very important to him to get married. He said that maybe he was old-fashioned, and maybe he was insecure, but he loved me and wanted to be married to me. That for him marriage meant commitment. And commitment felt like family.

"George's father died when he was a young boy. And his mother died last year. His kids aren't anywhere near us. I understood that it was important to him. And I also realized how much I care about his feelings. The idea of not being with him just seemed intolerable to me. It's not so much that I wasn't scared of marrying him. It's just that I was more scared of not having him in my life. If you want to call that priorities, call it priorities."

As soon as Kate was able to accept the fact that George was less than perfect—that he laughed too loudly—or that somebody might have disapproved of his behavior—she was able to relax in a whole new way in the relationship. In accepting George's limitations Kate was able to accept her own; in so doing her relationship with George became more human. It became a place she was able to simply *be*. She could be strong, weak, hip, gauche, naive, knowing, etc. And so could he.

There's an important difference, however, between accepting a man's full range of feelings and what has come to be called "settling." In each case, the action may be the same. Someone might have heard about Kate's decision to marry George and said, "Oh. I guess she finally decided to settle." Kate, however, doesn't feel that she has compromised by agreeing to marry George. The decision to accept someone —flaws and all—and the decision to "settle" for someone are motivated by different sets of feelings. And the difference is critical.

Had Kate continued to believe that George was a "schmuck" who didn't know how to behave at a party, but decided, "I just can't do any better," she would, indeed, have been "settling" or "lowering her standards." In that case she would have felt cheated. Instead, she made a decision based upon her emotional needs and as a result came out feeling good about herself and George.

When women feel as though they're "settling" for a man they express their disappointment in all sorts of ways. Some of them make jokes. "I had a date last week," one woman told us. "He wasn't Mr. Right, but he had a pulse." Other's feel that their poor showing reflects their own inadequacy. "I did the best I could," such a woman might say. Still others become cynical and bitter. And many of them channel their anger toward men. Kate, for example, who felt angry with George for laughing too loud, was able to recognize the limitations of that anger and move on to more productive feelings.

When women idealize men, they are, in effect, distancing themselves from them. The more unrealistically women see men—whether they see them as being too good, or too bad— the less likely they are to establish a genuinely close, trusting relationship. In idealizing men, women fall for the image they have created; they don't see the real person. And it is only with a real person that one can build an intimate relationship. If we're close to an image we feel empty. As we approach a real person we feel connected . . . happy, angry, disappointed, warm.

This issue of women's idealizing men is not unlike the issue of men idealizing women. When men held women up on pedestals, women felt, with good reason, that men didn't know who they really were. And beyond that, women felt that their relationships were built on a precarious foundation.

Kate still doesn't like the fact that George has a booming laugh. She still doesn't understand, entirely, why it bothers her as much as it does. She did make the effort to understand, however, why George wanted to marry her. And she also took the trouble to understand why he sometimes explodes with emotion when he leaves his office at the end of a long day. Essentially, she made an effort to understand the feelings behind George's actions and, as a result of that effort, she can allow herself the pleasure of continuing to love him.

"The truth is," Kate noted, "that I am a performer. It's very hard for me not to be *on*—not to be looking for feedback. Before I met George I was always involved with men who also had a need to be *on*, and George just put an end to that. He doesn't tolerate it. When I'm with him it's uncomfortable for me to be anything but honest about how I really feel. He cuts through all the bullshit just by putting his hand on my shoulder. That may sound nuts, but it's the truth. And I've come to realize that that quality of his is much more important for me than whether or not he comes across well at a party. That's the quality I can't risk losing."

The issue for Kate—and for all women as they come to terms with their great need for intimacy—is priorities. We'll discuss those priorities in greater detail in Chapter 9. Essentially, women need to ask themselves whether or not they are going to face up to their very human need for intimacy or continue to punish themselves by accepting an obsolete doctrine about what sort of relationships they *should* have with men.

The Prize

Probably the best motivation for struggling the way Kate did to focus on her feelings about George, rather than on appearances—to focus on internal, rather than external standards—is the loving-yet-open relationship she has with George. Kate and George have managed to supplant a traditional hierarchical relationship with one that allows room for two autonomous people while offering them real security. Let's look at both pieces of that prize.

AUTONOMY

When men and women develop relationships around internal, rather than external, criteria, they are, essentially, relieved of the burden of a hierarchy. Women have room to grow, in all the ways we've talked about, and so do men.

Marsha, a highly acclaimed contemporary artist, talked about her relationship with her husband Alex, a gifted and successful composer, in terms of autonomy.

"I think a lot of men like Alex, who were married previously to women who did not have careers—women who were totally dependent on them not only financially but even more so emotionally—I think that they found this too much of a burden. Many of them—in running off with younger women—have actually chosen women the second time around who are involved in their own work. The work, I think, is much more to the point than the age difference. I think that many men just feel like they can't stand the emotional pressure of having someone else living through them vicariously.

"I remember in the early days of our marriage," she said, "one day Alex was making a speech somewhere and I was with him. He said that it was a different experience for him to be with me in this sort of situation than it was for him to be with his first wife because I wasn't nervous about his speech. And I said," Marsha laughed, " 'Why in the world would I be nervous about *your* speech? I'm nervous enough about my own speeches, I don't need to be nervous about your speeches.'

"Of course, a wife who isn't making her own speeches and who is living totally through her husband is going to be nervous when he makes his speech. And I was able to understand that so clearly. I was reminded of how nervous kids are when they are in a school play. All children go through it. . . . They're nervous and their parents are nervous with them. And I remember what a terrible burden my parents' nervousness was on me. I felt like I not only had to do well for myself, but I had to do well for them also . . . for their emotional well-being. I always felt this conflict: I wanted them in the audience so that they'd be proud if I did well . . . but a piece of me wished they just weren't there."

SECURITY

Marsha and Alex have a security in their relationship that couples who are less autonomous don't have. If, for example, Alex delivers a dreadful speech, he doesn't have to be concerned about how it will influence Marsha's feelings for him. There is an inherent insecurity that comes when one focuses on accomplishment and appearance. "What if I stop achieving?" "What if I am less beautiful?" When you are balanced precariously on a pedestal, there is always, in the back of your mind, the concern that you might fall off.

These issues become particularly significant in long-term relationships as people age. Aside from the fact that physical appearance alters as we grow older, people must begin to deal with what they have and what they haven't accomplished. This sort of taking stock is, at best, difficult. When we are in relationships with people who can empathize, the road through those passages seems a bit less hazardous.

Sexuality, as we'll see in the next chapter, also changes over the course of a relationship.

CHAPTER 8

The Legacy of Female Sexuality

It's no mere coincidence that the Sexual Revolution and the Women's Movement occurred in the same historical moment. The two movements, from a woman's perspective, addressed the same issue: how women might gain access to what men had. The Women's Movement focused on women's desires for economic and social autonomy. The rallying cry was for equality. The Sexual Revolution—from a female point of view—focused on women's desire for pleasure. The rallying cry was for orgasms.

How had sexual pleasure eluded women? What had sex meant to women if not pleasure? What did today's career women learn about sex when they were children? How did their thinking differ from men's? What's the significance of that difference? And how does it continue to affect career women today?

In order to explore these questions we must return to the childhood AVBs we addressed earlier. The continuing impact of childhood attitudes, values, and behavior regarding sex is evident in much of what the women say throughout this book. When they say, for example, that they feel obligated to sleep with men whom they don't really want to sleep with, this sense of obligation has more to do with what they learned about sex as children than with their dates' manipulation. When the women you've been reading about say that they aren't physically turned on to the men they are meeting because they aren't the "right kind of guys," they're frequently manifesting childhood AVBs. And when women stay in relationships with men who treat them poorly because "We have a terrific chemistry in the sack," they too are manifesting childhood AVBs.

The reason is that what turns us on and off sexually is not a matter of "chemistry" or "magic" nearly so much as it is a matter of training.

All of the issues of power between men and women that we've discussed throughout this book have been played out, and continue to be played out, in the bedroom. Women were programmed very specifically when it came to sexual behavior, and those old programs are still in operation. Sometimes they are evident. Other times they're more oblique. But they always interfere with intimacy.

Early Lessons on Sex

The most critical difference between what boys and girls learned about sex revolves around the issue of pleasure.

Men grew up with the message that sex was supposed to be fun. It was something to be desired. It felt good. Indeed, adolescent boys who felt sexual desire were deemed "healthy," while boys who didn't were viewed with concern, and even suspicion. Clearly, men didn't need a social movement to tell them that the climax of sexual intercourse was supposed to be pure physical pleasure. The environment of their childhoods—their childhood AVBs—made the connection between sexuality and pleasure for them.

That link between sex and physical pleasure, however, was as distinctly masculine as was the link between sex and power—money—which we discussed in Chapter 2. Men owned these things and women's only hope of getting them was through men.

The link between sex and power has been successfully challenged by career women. But these same career women —as we'll see—are not yet convinced that they own their sexuality. They still believe that sexuality is something men must give them. And when we look at women's history regarding sex, it's no wonder.

Sex, as most girls grew up understanding it, had very little to do with pleasure. "I never wanted to fix my kid sister up with one of my friends," a young man explained, "because if he didn't have a good time with her I'd feel bad, and if he did have a good time with her I'd kill him." Clearly, the issue of his sister "having a good time" never even entered the picture.

"On one of my first dates," a forty-year-old pediatrician named Cathy M. recalled, "back when I was in high school, I went to a movie with a boy named Chuck, and when it was finished we drove to a cul-de-sac near the local cemetery. It was a famous place to park and neck. I'd never really made out with a boy before and I couldn't believe how much I liked it. Chuck began to undo my bra and I let him. I knew that anything above the waist was allowed. But I wasn't prepared for what I would feel when he began to play with my breasts. I didn't know it at the time, but my breasts are very sensitive. They're really an erogenous zone for me. I guess I must have made some noise—moaned or something—and Chuck suddenly stopped what he was doing. I didn't understand what was happening at the time, but I knew that I'd done something wrong. I was disappointed, but not surprised, when he didn't ask me out for the following weekend.

"A few days later I found out from the sister of one of Chuck's best friends that Chuck had asked me out thinking I was a 'nice' girl and wasn't interested in me when he found out I was 'easy.' He could go to a whore for that. In his opinion I was a 'slut.'

"I didn't understand. After all, I'd followed the rules. We never really *did* anything. He never touched me below the waist. What had I done that was wrong? It took me a long time to put it all together. Finally some of my friends helped. They said that Chuck had been telling people that I really liked *it*. That was my problem. I liked *it*. Nice girls weren't supposed to like *it*. I was supposed to either stop liking sex, or have the savvy to not show how much I liked it. What did I know? No man had ever played with my breasts before. I wasn't prepared for liking it so much, so how could I have been prepared for acting as if I didn't like it?"

As Cathy became more experienced with men, she learned to curb her sexual responses, both consciously and unconsciously. She learned—essentially—to be the kind of woman the man she was with wanted. "I really learned how to read a man sexually. I learned, for example, that most men don't like women to be too assertive sexually, so I never was. And I learned to be less eager. I guess you could say that I learned to put a cap on it. I'm not really all that sexual a person," Cathy admitted. "I put a lot of energy into my work and there isn't too much left when I get home." It seems that Cathy put a cap on her desire for sexual pleasure and hasn't yet learned how to take it off.

What did Cathy and women like her learn that sex meant for women if not pleasure? Women grew up with the understanding that sex had to do with enticement, with romance, and with obligation. These associations varied, as we'll see, depending upon whether or not a woman was married.

Premarital Sex

The most resounding message girls learned about sex before marriage was "Don't!" Virginity was paramount. What
was behind the taboo? The taboo against premarital sex for
women probably had its origins in biology. Before women
had reliable birth control, sexual intercourse meant the possibility of pregnancy, and, as we said earlier, women couldn't
afford to get pregnant without the economic support of a
man. But very early on, the issue of virginity became much
bigger for women than its origins. Indeed, virginity took on
religious proportions.

Young girls learned that sex was one of the few things for
which men needed them. And smart girls learned not to
squander so valuable an asset. Most of what girls absorbed
about sex before marriage involved learning how to "play
their cards," or "cast their bait." Today's career women grew
up understanding that it was healthy and right for them to
withhold sex from men until they got something—like the
promise of marriage—in return. For unmarried women, sex
was the primary means to security. "When I was about six,
my mother caught me dancing naked with the boy next
door," said Alice J., a thirty-six-year-old woman who heads up
her own catering service. "Bobby and I had been playing
that way for some time and the thing I remember most about
our time together was how good it felt. We used to rub
against each other and play with each other. We both really
loved it.

"When my mother found us she took me out of the room
and called for Bobby to get dressed and go home. I was really
scared about what she'd do. I mean, I was old enough to know
that I shouldn't have been naked with a boy. My mother was
absolutely ashen. 'How could you?' she demanded of me. 'It
feels good,' I said. She sat me down on her bed, and told me,

in this very serious voice, that if I did things like that with
Bobby, or anyone else, no man would ever want to marry me.
Then she walked out of the room and I cried and cried. I was
terrified. The whole scene remains vivid in my mind to this
day. I honestly believed that no one would marry me."

"Don't just give it away," girls were advised by their mothers and fathers. "Once a guy gets it," they warned, "he'll
drop you like a hot potato." "No man wants damaged goods."

There it was. Sex was fun for men and dangerous—damaging, even—for women. Alice's mother was teaching her
daughter two important lessons about sex just as she had
been taught them by her own mother. First, she was teaching her to disassociate sex from pleasure. And second, she
taught her to get something other than pleasure in exchange
for sex. Translation: a husband. She was handing down a
legacy that Alice is dealing with today in therapy.

"At work I feel my worth. I have confidence in who I am.
But in relationships I'm not so sure. Probably the most difficult thing for me," Alice confided, "is to really believe that a
man is interested in me for more than just sex. It's a terrible
problem, because when I sleep with a guy because I feel
pressured to I end up feeling angry. And when I don't sleep
with a guy the whole issue of sex becomes bigger and bigger
in my imagination and I feel like this stereotypical, manipu-
lating, conniving woman. That's an image I'm very uncomfortable with. I like to think of myself as up-front. That's the
way the people I work with think of me. Yet every time I go
out with a man I haven't slept with I spend my entire evening maneuvering the scenario and worrying about whether
or not we're going to end up in bed."

Not all women have as difficult a time as Alice with the
issue of using their sexuality to get things for themselves.
"When I know that a guy is attracted to me," Carla V., a real
estate broker, said, laughing, "I feel very powerful. All I have
to do is play my cards right and I can have him eating out of
the palm of my hand. I never sleep with men that I'm profes-

sionally involved with," Carla emphasized. "I hate the whole notion of women sleeping their way to the top. But I know for sure that I can drive a better deal when the man I'm dealing with finds me attractive. It gives me an extra edge."

Carla sounds cold and calculating, but the fact is that her point of view has more to do with powerlessness than it does with power. It reflects the sense of powerlessness most women grew up feeling vis-à-vis men. Without the promise of sex, Carla feels less powerful. The problem is evident in her personal life. "Once I've slept with a guy," Carla said, echoing Alice and many of the other women we interviewed, "I feel much less secure. I'm afraid he'll lose interest." Indeed, without the promise of sex, Carla feels devalued.

The "promise" feels more valuable to these women than the act itself, because the promise is where they experience their power, and their pleasure came more from experiencing that power than from sexual intercourse.

Conjugal Sex

Of course everything changed after marriage . . . but the change did not involve pleasure. Sex for the married woman primarily involved obligation. To be sure, on a conscious level sex might have meant more than obligation to many married women: It might have meant tenderness, or romance, or for some few women it might genuinely have meant physical pleasure, but those experiences were ancillary to obligation. Sex was a woman's "conjugal duty." After all, sexual availability was what they traded off for security, and women with integrity understood that they had to live up to their share of the bargain.

In the context of the kinds of hierarchical relationships we discussed earlier—relationships premised on the deference of women—a woman's deference in the bedroom was appropriate. "Females were supposed to inhibit aggression and open displays of sexual urges," wrote Harvard psychologist Jerome Kagan in an article entitled "Review of Child Development Research" (New York, Russell Sage Foundation, 1964). Instead, they were "to be passive with men, to be nurturant to others, to cultivate attractiveness. *To maintain an effectively socially poised and friendly posture with others.*"

In other words, women had to sublimate their sexual urges into "socially poised and friendly" behavior. It was part and parcel of being a woman . . . part of being feminine. In the context of their families and the world at large, "socially poised and friendly" behavior meant being "other-oriented." It meant defining yourself in terms of your relationships. In the bedroom this sublimation translated into treading the thin line between being ready, willing, and able to have sex with one's husband and being pushy or demanding. Women who wanted sex for themselves were labeled "demanding," or "masculine," or worse, "ball-busters."

In order for women to succeed at being other-oriented sexually, they had first to lose touch with their own sexual urges. Indeed, "smart" women went one step beyond not initiating sex. They didn't, to their knowledge, feel the sexual urges that would tempt them to initiate it. They were, however, ready, willing, and able to have sex with their husbands whenever *their husbands desired*. That availability made them "friendly." It made them feminine.

Women who went on to pursue ambitious careers learned, as we said earlier, to go after success in the workplace. They learned, for example, to say "I want to be a vice president in five years" and do what was necessary to realize their goals. But when these same women had to shift from being self-oriented in the workplace to other-oriented in the bedroom, they experienced either conflict, anger, inadequacy, or depression.

"I was married to the same man for fifteen years," says Rhonda F., an executive with an insurance company, "and I don't think I ever once, in all those years, came right out and initiated sex. It's not that I don't like sex. In fact, I thought our sex life was very good—it was the best part of our marriage. Usually when we had sex I enjoyed it. But I was just never comfortable saying 'Let's make love.' I'm a fairly aggressive woman, so it's not as though I don't feel comfortable asking for things or going after things I want. I do it all the time at work. But sex is different. As a matter of fact, I think I sort of took pride in the fact that I never had to ask for sex. Asking was Jack's job. Accepting was mine."

Beyond being sexually available, however, women were supposed to be sexually appreciative. In fact, the more they expressed appreciation of their husband's sexual prowess, the more feminine they were.

Expressing pleasure and *experiencing* pleasure, of course, are two very different things. It was women's efforts to be friendly—to please the men in their lives—that led them to lose touch with their own sexual urges. And women who were not in touch with their sexual feelings but who wanted to please their husbands did so by faking orgasms. Unfortunately, the effort involved in *faking* an orgasm makes it impossible for them to relax and have one.

"The pressures that have long made so many women forgo orgasm during lovemaking and fake orgasms during intercourse are real social pressures," Alix Shulman wrote in a collection of essays called *Woman in Sexist Society.* "The explanation that it is all simply a result of ignorance, men's and women's, will not do. Hopelessly isolated from each other in their cells in a male-dominated society, even with the facts around, women have still had to fake orgasm to keep their men, to hide their imagined or imputed inadequacy, to demonstrate 'love,' to gain a man's approval, to boost a man's ego, or, with orgasm nowhere in sight, to get the man please to stop."

The sexual deference of women was reinforced by the institutions of our culture. Until recently there was no crime of rape between husband and wife. In other words, women had no legal right to refuse to have sex with their husbands. Indeed, it wasn't until 1980 that New York State passed a law specifying that where a husband and wife were *legally separated* the wife had a right to charge her husband with rape.

The consequences of women having been "other-oriented," rather than "pleasure-oriented," in the bedroom were profound. Essentially, women were trained to be responsive to men's sexual urges at the expense of noticing their own. Women's sexual urges took on value during the 1960s and 1970s, however, when a confluence of factors led women to examine and ultimately reject the sexual AVBs of their childhoods.

First contraception—which was at the heart of the sexual revolution—freed women to begin thinking about what they might get from sex . . . other than pregnant. Reliable contraception meant that women were freed of a burden, and without that burden they could begin thinking about sex as a source of pleasure. Second, women began to pursue things that historically had been accessible only to men, and sexual pleasure was precisely such a thing. Third, in the wake of the Sexual Revolution, Madison Avenue had inextricably connected "sexiness" with "success." And career women, more than most, cared about projecting a "successful" image. It was "in" to be sexy. This new "sexy career woman" image was quite different from the old "sexless career gal" image we discussed in Chapter 2, and everyone was aware of the difference: women at work as well as women at home.

The very same women who had been suppressing their sexual desire for most of their lives began, for the first time, to look for it. The problem for many of these women was that their training had been too well reinforced by the culture in which they lived for them to break out of their old patterns. Many women had been other-directed for so long that they'd simply lost touch with their own feelings. Learning to notice their sexual urges was no small task. Learning what to do with those urges—learning to associate sexuality with pleasure and then to pursue that pleasure—was more difficult still.

Owning Your Own Sexuality

Those same childhood AVBs that once fostered women's feelings of inadequacy in the workplace, fostered feelings of sexual inadequacy in women as well. Although women today have managed to replace those childhood AVBs with adult/masculine AVBs as far as the workplace is concerned, they have not been able to make the switch where their sexuality is concerned. Many of today's career women still don't recognize that their sexuality—their capacity for passion—lies within themselves. They hold on—often unconsciously—to their other-oriented childhood belief that they need men to *make them* sexual.

It's important here to make a distinction between needing men for sex, and needing men to feel sexual. Heterosexual men and women need each other for sexual relationships. Autonomous men and women, however, each come to those relationships with their own sexuality in order to *share* their passion with each other. Women who don't own their own sexuality rely on men to make them feel sexual—to *give* it to them. We will elaborate on the difference between "sharing" and "giving and taking" in Chapter 9. For now, it's enough to say that "sharing" implies mutuality and autonomy. "Giving and taking" implies dependence and deference.

Let's look at some of the ways women who say they're sexual, in fact, aren't.

He Makes Me Feel Like a Natural Woman

Paula F. is one such woman.

For the fifteen years that Paula has been married to Ed,

their sex life has been erratic and unsatisfying. "We were both so young when we met," explained Paula, a thirty-five-year-old insurance executive. "I think the extent of Ed's experience was kissing another girl before he met me during our freshman year at college. The first time we actually had intercourse was our wedding night and I can tell you that I didn't hear any bells.

"And I never have . . . that is, I never have with Ed. Somehow, work became very consuming for both of us. I was putting in twelve-hour days before I became an executive. When I came home I was too tired to think about sex. I think, over the years, Ed made an adjustment. At least, he never pushed the issue with me. At one point four months went by without our having sex. Ed would sometimes try to initiate sex during that period but it just never worked. He just didn't seem to know how to make me feel sexy.

"A few months ago," Paula continued in a very matter-of-fact tone of voice, "I began having an affair with a client. Even before we went to bed we had both felt a very strong sexual attraction. About two weeks after we met, Bruce asked me to lunch. And over coffee he said outright that he found me very attractive and wanted to take me to bed. I remember feeling incredibly excited—physically I felt this fullness between my legs—and I also was frightened. I told him that I was married and that I'd never been unfaithful, but that I found him very attractive. I said that I needed some time to think. At that point he put his hand under the table and touched my thigh and said, 'This has nothing to do with thinking.'

"We left the restaurant, got into a cab, and went directly to his apartment. And we proceeded to make love for the entire afternoon. I didn't even call my office to say I'd be out for the rest of the day. The whole experience was beyond my imagination. I mean, for more than fifteen years—for my whole life, really—I had never had an orgasm. True, I am married to an extremely good-looking, sweet, kind man who loves me.

And in many ways I love him. But I've never had an orgasm. Not one.

"Then, in one afternoon with a near stranger, I somehow become this multiorgasmic woman. I just couldn't stop. At one point we were lying in bed . . . having a respite . . . and Bruce began to play with my nipple. He kept at it for maybe ten minutes, and I was going crazy. Finally, he moved his hand from my breast to between my legs and in an instant I just exploded.

"That night when I got home, at about nine, I felt like I wanted to conduct a scientific experiment. So I let Ed know that I wanted to make love. And, of course, it was the same as it had always been. Basically nothing. Which leaves me in a quandary. Bruce makes me come alive sexually. When I'm with him I know I don't have any sexual hang-ups. It all really works. With Ed, I have a nice life. He cares for me. Our daughter thinks he's probably the best father in history, and I think she's right. But he makes me feel sexless.

"So I'm caught in this affair which involves lying to my husband, which is something I hate doing. But I can't stop seeing Bruce. It's the old line about not knowing what you've missed until you have it. Now that I've been with a man who makes me feel sexual, I have a harder time than before going without sex."

Paula, in keeping with her childhood AVBs, attributes her sexuality to the man she's with. Ed makes her feel sexless. Bruce makes her feel multiorgasmic. She is frustrated and angry in her relationship with Ed because he isn't giving her passion—and she wants it. She feels dependent in her relationship with Bruce because she believes that he alone has the key to her passion. That dependency will, as history bears out, ultimately lead to anger as well.

The fact is that Paula is not having an affair with Bruce because she wants to share her passion. She's having it because she needs to prove to herself that she doesn't have sexual problems and Ed does. Her affair with Bruce is more about success than it is about pleasure. Paula goes home to have sex with Ed for the same reason. She's conducting an experiment, the goal of which is her own vindication.

As long as Paula allows men to "give" her sex, however, she also allows them to take it away. What would happen to Paula's sexuality if Bruce eventually lost interest in her? Her precarious sexual self-image would be shattered. If Bruce makes Paula come alive, he can also make her feel dead.

Women, of course, have long been taught to relinquish control of their lives to men. It's nothing new for women to deny themselves their sexuality. It's interesting, however, that women who have struggled so successfully to gain economic independence from men should still believe—on an emotional, if not an intellectual, level—that they are helpless and at the mercy of men for their passion.

When Paula begins to recognize that her desires and passions are not given to her by men—that they are as much a part of who she is as her arms and legs—she'll be in a better position to do her part in working out some of the problems she and Ed have in bed. The issue is one of expectations. When Paula stops feeling that it's Ed's responsibility to *make her come alive sexually,* she'll feel less victimized by his inability to do so. Consequently, she'll feel less angry with him . . . less eager to point an accusing finger. With the anger aside, she may notice her own passion and be able to share it. Or she may notice her lack of passion and perhaps ask why she doesn't feel anything.

The Turn-On

Many of the single women we interviewed had the same problem as Paula but expressed it differently. "I met a guy a few months ago who was exactly the kind of guy I should be involved with," a woman named Irene told us, "but he just didn't turn me on." As soon as Irene thinks in terms of "should," she becomes hostage to her childhood AVBs. Those AVBs block the possibility that Paula might develop her own adult criteria based upon an understanding of her own needs. She thinks she's rejecting her childhood AVBs by not feeling passion toward the "right kind of men." In fact, rejection is an indication of involvement, albeit a negative involvement. Her need to reject men she thinks of as suitable according to her childhood AVBs is a good barometer of her continued involvement with those attitudes, values, and behavior. Her own personal assessment of each person and what they have to offer is still missing.

"Tom is a real bastard," commented a woman named Maureen about a man she was dating, "but we've got great chemistry in bed. What can I say? The guys I have the best time with in bed are usually bastards on any other level." Maureen can only enjoy sex when she is being punished—when she has it with a "bastard." She has internalized a message that says she should not experience sexual pleasure. Consequently, when she does experience her own passion she must be punished.

The women we interviewed were hardworking, logical, intelligent people with a solid base in reality. They would never, for example, entrust their health to the care of a witch doctor. Yet when it comes to sex they speak unabashedly of magic, of karma, and of chemistry. (Chemistry, in this context, has less to do with science than it does with the unknown.) All of this talk of magic is significant. Historically people have attributed to magic things they think are beyond their control. Women who couch their sexuality in terms of the occult are, essentially, disowning it.

Marge K. is one such woman. "Look," explains this thirty-eight-year-old lawyer. "I'm willing to give a nice guy the old college try, but the fact is that I just don't lubricate with some guys and I do with others." The problem is that the men who turn Marge on are by her own judgment the wrong kind of men. "I'm very turned on by powerful men, and most men

who are into power are not the kind of guys I'd want to make
my life with. What am I supposed to do about that. Sex isn't a
lot of fun when I'm dry."

Marge rests her case. After all, the magic is supported by
scientific evidence. It's beyond refute. She lubricates for
some men and doesn't for others. In the face of such evidence Marge believes she has two options: She can either
date the men who turn her on, or have a sexually unsatisfying
relationship with a man who doesn't.

There is, of course, another option. Marge can think about
the criteria for selecting a man that we discussed earlier and
begin to examine why she is so attracted to power. What does
that attraction tell her about herself? There's no question
that all women find some men more attractive than others.
But who they find attractive and who they don't find attractive—all of the talk about chemistry and magic—has much
more to do with women's heads than with their genitals.

Vaginas function—or don't function—in conjunction with
women's heads. When their heads allow them to feel turned
on to someone, their vaginas respond. They get wet. When
their heads shut someone out, their vaginas shut them out as
well.

We don't suggest that sex is an intellectual matter. Good
sex involves feeling—not thinking. But the things that turn
people on are the things they value or feel they need or want.
Marge is turned on to power because she doesn't feel powerful herself. She knows, however, that the feelings of power
she gets from being connected to a powerful man are tenuous at best. That sort of power is not real. Before Marge can
feel turned on to the kind of men she thinks she can really
build a life with, she'll have to deal with her own feelings of
impotence.

Women's Pursuit of Pleasure

As women came to realize that they were no longer sub-servient to men's needs, wishes, and desires—that any activity they engaged in should have something in it for them directly—their expectations of sex changed as well. "Is sex to be pleasurable only for men, or is it to be pleasurable for me too?" they asked. And, of course, it didn't take very long for them to figure out that they too could experience pleasure. And they went out looking for it.

But women didn't really have models on which to base their new sexual ambitions, any more than they had role models on which to base their career ambitions. Indeed, the only people upon whom women could model their pursuit of sexual pleasure were men. And that's precisely what they did. They rejected their traditional female AVBs and adapted the traditional male AVBs. The reasoning was that if they wanted what men had (i.e., sexual pleasure) they'd have to act like men. It was the same reasoning they had used in the workplace and, as you'll see, it had the same shortcomings.

Women discovered in bed, just as they discovered in the workplace, that they were not men, and therefore, they were not comfortable assuming men's attitudes, values, and be-havior. They did, of course, discover lust and passion, and that was an important discovery. But women came to passion with other needs as well. Specifically, women came to sexual-ity with the need for emotional contact. And the stereotypi-cal male didn't address that need.

"I was in a women's consciousness-raising group in the early 1970s," Felice S., a thirty-nine-year-old network execu-tive, told us, "and the big thing everyone talked about was sex and masturbation. We all tried to support each other's efforts to have orgasms. The fact is that we were all incredi-bly horny and rather inexperienced.

"It was about that time that I started becoming pretty promiscuous. I was like a kid let loose in a candy store. I wanted to do everything. Try everything. And I was greedy to have my orgasms. It didn't matter so much whom I slept with. If a man could sleep around, so could a woman. I had lots of one-night stands and talked with my women friends about how good in bed this man was and how terrible that one was. I felt I could be as casual about sex as the next guy.

"The truth is," Felice concluded, "that I wasn't having all that great a time. I mean, I was having orgasms, but I wasn't really having fun. I began to hate waking up next to guys I didn't know. I was tired. It didn't feel like an adventure anymore. In fact, it became very boring. I started to feel like I'd do better to stay home and masturbate than to sleep with some of the men I slept with. The truth was that I wanted more continuity in my life. And most of my friends had similar feelings."

As we said earlier, women cannot simply drop their own childhood AVBs and assume the AVBs of men. It doesn't work in bed any better than it works in the workplace. Instead, they need to go out and find the kind of sexuality that is right for them. The issue really involves learning to let go of control more than it involves seizing control.

Seizing Control Vs. Letting It Go

There is a difference between letting go of control, which is necessary for good sex, and seizing control. When women like Felice first began to pursue their own sexual pleasure they felt the need to seize control of sex. They had gone without sexual pleasure for so long that they were hungry for it. "Give me," women began saying in bed. "Give me what's mine!" "Touch this!" "Squeeze that!" "Harder!" "Not so soft!"

Women had suffered as a result of men's controlling sex and the most logical antidote was for them to control it themselves. But when women first realized that they could ask for what they wanted in bed, many of them turned into three-star generals. For a little while the excitement of that new control was fulfilling; but ultimately, women didn't feel any more satisfaction as generals than they did as buck privates.

The bedroom was simply not a place for rank. Women soon recognized that when they seized control of sex the resulting dynamic was not all that different from what it was when men were in control. As long as they maintained the distance necessary in any chain of command, the closeness they longed for continued to elude them. They continued to have sex without contact.

Letting go of control sexually involves an opening up—both physically and emotionally. And that sort of opening up usually requires trust. It involves saying to yourself, "I'm going to feel whatever I feel at a given moment. If I feel passionate, I'm not going to stop myself. If I don't feel passionate I'm not going to pretend I do." The ability to let go of control in this way is no small task for women. We talked earlier about owning your own sexuality. In order to let go of control sexually women must not only own their own sexuality, they need to notice it as well.

Noticing Sexuality

"What do you do when you feel sexual?" we asked. "I try not to notice," quipped Loretta K., a thirty-seven-year-old editor. "Frankly, for years, when I was younger, I'd go to a bar and find myself someone to sleep with. Now that I've rejected that sort of casual sex—which never left me feeling very good—I've pretty much stopped feeling sexual. What do I do when I have a sexual urge?" she asked herself. "I guess I put a lid on it."

When Loretta "puts a lid on" her sexual urges she doesn't eradicate them. She simply "puts" them somewhere she won't notice them. Her sexuality, however, still exists buried inside her. Loretta, and many other women who cannot seem to find sexually fulfilling intimate relationships, would rather *not notice* their sexuality than notice it and feel frustrated. The problem is that women who spend years actively "not noticing" their sexual urges have a difficult time believing, on an emotional level, that they are sexual. They don't really believe that they own their sexuality. Indeed, women who "put a lid on" their sexual urges are most often the same women who believe that men have the power to "make" them sexual.

"Well what am I supposed to do?" Loretta asked. "If I let myself feel every sexual urge I'd be in a constant state of frustration." The truth is that on an unconscious level Loretta is probably more frustrated when she denies her sexual urges than she would be if she acknowledged them and acted on them.

Acting on a sexual urge need not mean going to a bar, picking up a stranger, and engaging in sexual intercourse. It might mean simply *feeling* the sexual urge. Sexual urges feel good, and women need not deny themselves the pleasure of those feelings simply because they are not going to follow through.

"When I feel a sexual urge and I'm at the office I think I become a bit flirtatious," explained Jennifer V., broker on Wall Street. "I used to just button it up, but then I realized that flirting was pretty much harmless. And fun. I like feeling sexy and relating to the people around me from that feeling. Of course I don't act inappropriately. I don't go around stroking people or coming on to them. It's much more subtle than that. And I like it."

When Jennifer flirts, she is, indeed, acknowledging her own feelings of sexuality; and that acknowledgment is what makes her feel good. Jennifer is, in effect, saying, "I am sexual." She is, as we discussed earlier, owning her sexuality and, as a result, she feels good. Beyond feeling good, however,

Jennifer's recognition of her own sexuality makes her both independent and attractive. The fact that Jennifer owns her own sexuality means that she has something to offer men. Rather than engaging with a man and hoping that he'll make her come alive sexually, Jennifer can approach a man as an independently sexual person and perhaps offer to share her passion.

When women notice their sexual urges they can do any number of things. They can masturbate. They can fantasize. They can call up a lover and say, "I've been thinking about you and can't wait to get home tonight." The point of taking notice is to take possession. Career women have learned to own other feelings that once were alien to them. They've learned to feel competent in the workplace. They've learned to feel worthy of powerful positions and high salaries. When they learn to own their sexuality—when they learn to believe emotionally that they are sexual and permitted to enjoy their sexuality—then they can think about finding fulfilling, egalitarian relationships like the ones we will describe in Chapter 9.

Part IV

RELATIONSHIPS

CHAPTER 9

Intimacy

The Need for Adult Families

A great deal of research has been done on the need children have for families, and for the loving attention and care that come with families. Study after study seem to indicate that infants who are deprived of stroking and holding when they are young don't thrive either emotionally or physically as a result. It's interesting, however, to note that all of the talk about the need for an intimate, nurturing environment focuses on children. Children need nurturing. Children need the ongoing, reassuring presence of familiar adults. Children need stroking and comforting and holding.

We don't take issue with any of that research. We do take issue, however, with where it stops. For some reason very little attention has been paid to the need people have for family once they have grown into adults. Indeed, there has been much more emphasis on the value of separating from one's family, as a sort of rite of passage into adulthood, than on the value of creating a similarly nurturing environment for oneself as an adult.

The fact is that we all have a need for the nurturing environment of a family when we are young, when we are old, and for all the years in between. That need for what we call "adult family"—which can, but certainly need not, involve children—doesn't have anything to do with economics or social status. Rather, it meets a basic human need, like hunger, which is pretty much the same for everyone: adults and children, men and women, executives and secretaries. People don't outgrow their need to be stroked and held; to be comforted when they are in pain; and to have someone they can run to with good news. Indeed, people need to be nurturing as much as they need to be nurtured. They need to be in a place where they can be tender, as much as they need to be treated tenderly.

People, quite simply, need an opportunity to replace the family in which they were raised and create a new safe harbor for themselves. They need the consistent presence of someone with whom they can chart their lives: the small, day-to-day happenings as well as the big events. Children need to know that there will be someone there when they come home from school or go to bed at night, someone to whom they can divulge the happenings of the day. And adults need the very same thing. If their childhood family was a good one, their adult family becomes a place to duplicate those good things from an adult perspective. If their childhood family was not a good one, their adult family presents them with a second opportunity.

Adults don't die when they're deprived of the sort of intimacy an "adult family" can provide, but they do suffer considerably. That suffering is evident in many of the women we've written about thus far. They feel emotionally isolated without the presence of an intimate partner to hear them from day to day and year to year. And their emotional isolation ultimately fosters withdrawal, ~~depression,~~ and insecurity.

Marriage: What It Was Supposed to Be and What It Was

We said at the beginning of this book that for earlier generations of women marriage was the means by which they took care of themselves: economically, emotionally, and sexually. It was for a long time their only option; but it has become less and less satisfying for women on all three accounts. Economic dependence resulted in hierarchical relationships which, over the course of time, became adversarial in nature. The link between economic dependence and sex made sex more obligatory than pleasurable. And the feeling of being economically trapped and sexually obligated precluded the possibility of the kind of nurturing, trusting, supportive adult family we discussed earlier. Indeed, over the last decade many women have turned out to be very disappointed in their marriages.

The Women's Movement began, in large part, as a response to the failure of traditional marriages. Women were energized by their dissatisfaction with traditional marriages to explore other options. They sought to free themselves from men economically by pursuing their own significant work; and when they left their homes for the workplace they discovered that they could manage, as free agents, to see to their own economic well-being. They pursued sexual satisfaction with comparable energy and found a new kind of pure physical pleasure once they were able to separate sex from obligation. They turned to friends—to other women—for the kind of nurturing support they were unable to get from men in the context of a traditional marriage, and they found that women could, indeed, offer each other emotional sustenance.

As women began to realize these new options they also began to look at marriage more critically. Women didn't need it for sex; they didn't need it for money; and, they thought, they didn't need it for emotional support. Indeed, from the perspective of these new options marriage began to look more like an encumbrance than a Shangri-la.

"A woman without a man," one popular slogan in the early days of the Women's Movement read, "is like a fish without a bicycle." "What do we need men for?" women were asking, and the question both frightened and excited them. "Now that we don't *have* to be with men, why should we *choose* to be with men?"

Men, meanwhile, were beginning to worry over that very same question. "What does she need me for?" asked a forty-eight-year-old man when his wife, who pursued a career designing children's clothing after her kids left high school, suddenly "hit it big." "All of a sudden she's filled with this overwhelming enthusiasm and energy. Here I am beginning to think about retiring, and my wife is taking off like a rocket on a new career. She works all hours, doesn't care much about the house, isn't really available to me when I want her, and doesn't seem very satisfied with what I have to offer . . . in bed, or anywhere else. I feel like a vestigial organ."

Men and women had built relationships on a foundation of economic dependency for so long that when the foundation began to shift it seemed as though the entire structure might collapse. And, indeed, when the collapse came—as it did for many people—it took a while for the dust to settle. For many years the air between men and women was too thick with anger and suspicion for either of them to see what it was that they needed from each other.

Recently, however, the air between men and women has begun to clear, and as they both begin to feel more comfortable with women's separateness, they are discovering that they need long-term commitments with each other for the same thing. They don't need long-term commitments in order to have economic security; and they don't need long-term commitments in order to have sexual fulfillment. But they do need long-term committed relationships in order to make "adult families." Essentially, they need each other for intimacy. And the kind of intimacy that heterosexual men and women can have with each other is very different from the kind that women can have between themselves.

Intimate Relationships

Our definition of an "intimate relationship" is, intentionally, quite specific. We chose our words carefully in order to differentiate an "intimate relationship" from the concepts of "love" and "marriage" that were part of everyone's childhood AVBs. When we talk about "intimacy" we mean an *egalitarian* relationship between two *autonomous* people in which both *focus on feelings,* more than on accomplishments.

EGALITARIAN

By "egalitarian," we do not mean an equal distribution of labor, or an equal responsibility for income. Egalitarianism regarding things that can be measured—tangible things like money and productivity—has more to do with traditional hierarchical relationships and childhood AVBs than with intimacy. Rather, we are concerned with an *emotional egalitarianism.* We are talking about relationships in which people acknowledge, from the start, that they each have strengths and weaknesses; that it's acceptable for each to acknowledge their vulnerabilities; and that the relationship will provide them each with succor. This sort of egalitarian relationship is, of course, significantly different from the "love" and "marriage" relationships that evolved from childhood AVBs. It is not hierarchical, therefore it is more supportive than adversarial in nature. No one is limited by old gender definitions to a position of strength or weakness. Egalitarian relationships are not based upon what people can give or take from each other so much as they're based on a willingness to share.

When relationships are not emotionally egalitarian, one person—usually the man—is up; another—usually the woman—is down. In such relationships partners can either give, or they can take. For our purposes, it doesn't matter who is giving and who is taking. What's important is understanding and recognizing the system in which one person *has* and another person *needs*. It is this system—a power system rather than a sharing system—that interferes with intimacy. It was this giving and taking—even if the man was giving diamonds and minks—that left women feeling isolated in their marriages.

In our culture *giving* is a patrician concept. Implicit in *giving* is the recognition that one is rich enough to give. The giver is in a position of power. Traditionally women, by *taking* from men, have assumed the role of dependent child; and men, by *giving* to women have asserted their positions of power. Maimonides recognized the power play of *giving* and *taking* more than eight hundred years ago when he set guidelines for the giving of charity. The most honorable way to give, according to those guidelines, was for the donor and the recipient to remain anonymous to each other.

As long as women continue to look for relationships rooted in their childhood AVBs—as long as they continue to look for the kind of "perfect men" they described in Chapter 6— their criteria for selecting men will reflect their need to either get or give. Accordingly, they will find men who can *give*, but who require "their women" to be psychologically dependent; or they will find men who can *take*, but who are psychologically dependent on them. Which of those two positions you are in usually depends on your innermost perception of yourself.

Think back to what the women we've discussed so far have been looking for in a man. They want men who are strong (i.e., tall, muscular, healthy, etc.), who are directed and ambitious, who like their work and want to continue doing it, who are rich or who aspire to becoming rich, and who will reflect well on them. Essentially, as we said earlier, they wanted men who could—one way or another—give those things to them. These same women begin to run into problems, however, because under these circumstances as soon as they *accept* those things from men, they set into motion an untenable hierarchy.

Intimate relationships—the kind of relationships women and men both need—are premised on *sharing*, rather than giving and taking. Both people come into the relationship acknowledging their emotional vulnerability. They need each other. They both begin in the same place in that regard. They both need to hold and be held. The dynamic of a sharing relationship, on the other hand, is one of *mutuality* rather than *adversarial*. No one is up, and no one is down.

Sharing, by this definition, must involve a gradual letting go of control, or opening up, and a willingness to lay your needs on the table even if you make yourself feel vulnerable in the process. It should be clear now why "trust" is a critical criteria in picking a partner. The issue is "Can I *trust* him with my innermost feelings?" He shouldn't have to resolve your problems, but he should respond to them with tenderness. (That's a critical distinction we'll develop in Chapter 10.)

"Letting go of control" and acknowledging vulnerability is, as we said earlier, particularly difficult for ambitious, career women because they see vulnerability as the opposite of strength, and they attribute their success to their strength. Vulnerability, for these women, was a handicap to be overcome, and it's not a feeling they're eager to get back in touch with. "If he knew that I threw up before I went to court," said a successful trial lawyer when she spoke of a new relationship, "he'd think I was crazy. He thinks I'm very together."

In the context of an adversarial, hierarchical relationship her fear is a valid one. If the balance of powers is critical to their relationship, acknowledging such feelings as fear, self-doubt, and neediness would be threatening. Relationships that are premised on egalitarianism, however, are not adversarial. In such relationships the acknowledgment of vulnerability requires courage and strength.

Nina, a forty-year-old managerial consultant, has the intellectual insight to identify her inability to share (translation: to let go of control) as a contributing factor in the dissolution of her eighteen-year marriage—but she lacks the necessary emotionality to turn herself around in terms of what she looks for in a new relationship.

"I have very little trouble giving," she said sadly, "but I do have trouble sharing. I'm really very good when it comes to giving gifts. When I give gifts—real material gifts or hugs and kisses and all that emotional stuff—it's just me making the effort. I'm doing something I choose to do and can recognize it as my own act . . . an act I'm in control of. Since I'm very geared to excelling, and always have been, I'm an excellent giver. Yet the idea of really sharing—letting go with another person—terrifies me. I've always had trouble having orgasms with Steve, probably because it requires that same sort of letting go and trusting. I'm not very good at trusting someone unless I'm in control. And I guess as long as I *am* in control I'm not really trusting." She laughed nervously. "It's a real problem."

Her insights, although remarkably on target, lack their corresponding emotional connections. She understands that she has difficulty sharing, but doesn't understand how this difficulty affects her relationships with men. After eighteen years in an unsatisfying relationship, she is beginning a new one that is destined for the same fate. As we listened to what she said about her new lover, it was clear that despite a change of roles, the dynamics of this new relationship still involve giving and taking, rather than sharing.

"Elliot," her new lover, "is very different from Steve," she explained with enthusiasm. "With Steve, I was always the one responsible for any kind of intellectual pursuit. I mean, he didn't really read very much, he wasn't interested in theater or music. If we went to the ballet, it was because *I* went out and got tickets. I think the problem goes all the way back to the beginning of our relationship. We were in college together, and whenever we both took the same course I always got the higher grade. I don't mean to sound egotistical, but I'm just more intelligent than Steve, and that always bothered me. He's a very sweet, gentle man, but he didn't really offer me any challenges. I mean there was nothing for me to strive toward in our relationship.

"Elliot, on the other hand, knows about so much: literature, art, even sports. I feel that I can learn a lot from him. He's always so interesting. I'd go so far as to say that Elliot is brilliant."

Nina has moved from a relationship in which she perceived herself as a "giver" to one in which she perceives herself as a "taker." She has not moved from a hierarchical relationship to an egalitarian one, however. Which leads us to ask what Nina expects to gain from Elliot's brilliance. When Nina said that Elliot gives her new standards to which she can aspire, she was really talking about competition. "Aspiring" and "competing" have nothing to do with intimacy.

Based on Nina's own analysis she has very little reason to feel sanguine about her future with Elliot. First of all, why should she assume that he will feel differently about her than she did about Steve? As someone who had difficulty loving a man whose IQ was perceived as lower than her own, Nina is not too likely to feel secure in a relationship in which she perceives her own IQ as lower. And suppose she "strives" intellectually and finally reaches a point where she thinks she's as smart or smarter than Elliot. What's to keep the relationship from self-destructing? And finally, how safe or content can one feel in a relationship that is based on striving and competition?

Would Nina, for example, be able to handle a blemish on Elliot's image? She might discover that despite his high IQ he is unable to relate to her children in a tender way. She might discover that despite his high IQ he is uninterested in what she has to offer. She might find herself unable to recognize and respond to Elliot's vulnerabilities. Intimacy doesn't require a matching-up of IQs. It has to do with two people who are in a relationship for the same reasons. If two people are smart enough to respond to each other's emotional needs, then they're smart enough to be in a relationship.

What Nina needs is a man who can recognize how frightened she is of "letting go" and be sympathetic to that problem. Elliot might be such a man, but if he is, Nina hasn't noticed.

AUTONOMOUS

We talked earlier about the fact that women traditionally had to abandon their identities to the men in their lives. On the most literal level, when Jane Smith married John Doe she became Mrs. John Doe. The emotional equivalent involved Jane's transition from being "Jane" to being "John's wife" and "John Jr.'s mother."

 Intimate relationships, as we describe them, require two *separate* people, with two *separate* sets of emotions, capabilities, interests, etc. But even more important, intimate relationships require that the people involved accept each other's autonomy.

When we discuss problems of autonomy they often appear, at first, to be trivial, revolving around such issues as appearance. When people focus on appearance instead of feelings, however, it means that they still believe, on some level, that their identity will come from their lover—that they will be seen in his reflection. And women should, by now, recognize the danger of that kind of situation.

Jane K., a forty-one-year-old financial planner, is distressed by the fact that she cannot find a man. Her sense of failure was heightened recently because Betty, one of her best friends, "found someone."

"I hadn't met Jim," Jane explains, referring to Betty's boyfriend. "They'd pretty much kept to themselves. But I heard all about him, and despite the fact that I was jealous, I was very happy for Betty. I mean, he sounded just great. Then last weekend she had a dinner party and I got to meet him. And I'll tell you, I was shocked when I saw him.

"Betty," Jane goes on, "is really beautiful. I mean, she's tall, and she's got a great body, and she really puts herself together well. She just always looks gorgeous. And there was Jim, this middle-aged, short, dumpy-looking guy." Jane's voice seems to gain strength as she focuses on detail. "I remember being really surprised at something Jim was wearing." She stops and tries to recall, and then remembers, "Oh, right. He had on these very wonky shoes—black crepe-soled shoes with white socks slipping down over his heel.

"The thing is," Jane continues, unwilling to move away from the subject of Betty and Jim and her surprise, "that they really seemed to be in love. They kept finding reasons to touch each other. And they were so eager to help each other out." She pauses and reaches for a cigarette. "I don't know. I mean, I don't think I'd ever even consider a second date with a guy who looked like such a nerd . . . and here's my best friend in love with him. What's wrong with me? I feel so deprived. Am I expecting too much?"

The issue for Jane isn't really whether or not she wants too much or not enough so much as what it is she expects from a relationship. Why does Jane care about how the man in her life dresses? She is shocked by the question, but attempts to answer it.

"I don't understand," she begins, and she is telling the

truth. She doesn't understand why her concern with how a man dresses is a problem. It seems to her to be the most natural concern in the world. "If I'm going to be seen with someone I want them to look good. I want to be proud of them. I don't want to be ashamed."

Of what would Jane be ashamed if she were seen with a man who looked like Jim? "Well," she says, "I guess I'd feel that people might think I couldn't do better."

Better than what? "Better than a guy who looks like a nerd."

Jane, of course, wants a man whose appearance will label her a success by the standards of her childhood AVBs. She doesn't want to "settle." The problem is that by focusing on appearances she is neglecting to take care of her emotional needs, and as a result, she experiences deprivation. Betty does not feel deprived. Jim, despite his funny shoes/socks/body, is there for Betty at night when everyone else has gone home. And apparently Jim is able to meet the emotional criteria we discussed earlier: He is tender, well intentioned, and worthy of Betty's trust.

When people see Betty and Jim together they register that they seem to be in love, and they may, or may not, register that Jim doesn't dress well. But suppose, in fact, Jim doesn't dress well. What does his poor taste in clothing mean . . . beyond the fact that he has poor taste in clothing? Jane seems to think that it means Jim is less valuable as a person, and that his lesser value will somehow rub off on her. Her problem comes when she begins to attach this kind of significance to Jim's mode of dress. When she begins to believe that his mode of dress reflects on her. Why, for example, should Jane focus on how the man in her life dresses when she is perfectly capable of projecting the image of a well-dressed, successful woman for herself?

When Jane is able to see the man in her life as a separate entity, she'll feel less concerned about how he reflects on her. She might be able to say, for example, "Jim is such an awful dresser and I, obviously, am someone who takes great pains with my wardrobe. We must look like the odd couple together. People must realize that we have something special going for us." Rather than, "Jim is such an awful dresser. People will think there's something wrong with me for being involved with him."

The difference is significant. Many of the women we spoke with focused on things like how men dressed, or how they decorated their apartments. And in each case the question they needed to ask was "How does his dressing/esthetic sensibilities/etc. affect his ability to share with me in an intimate relationship?" We didn't hear any answers that convincingly addressed that question.

FOCUSING ON FEELINGS

The last part of our definition of an intimate relationship involves the issue of focusing on "feelings" rather than actions. Focusing on feelings means attempting to understand the emotions that trigger someone's actions, rather than simply "reacting" to his actions. It isn't always an easy thing to do, and it isn't always one's first impulse, but it *is* terribly important. Focusing on feelings, rather than actions, is what makes an intimate relationship safe. It's a great comfort to know that someone cares enough about you to consider the motivations behind your actions.

It is at this point in a relationship that trust and goodwill become important. Consider the following situation.

Emily G., a thirty-two-year-old engineer, went out with a man she liked very much. They'd seen each other two or three times when he began pressuring her to go to bed with him. He—Adam—had just ended a five-year relationship and was very eager to have sex with another woman. Emily didn't know how to handle his pressure. "If I were in my office," she explained, "and someone got grabby or grubby, I'd just tell them to get lost. And that was my impulse with

Adam. I was angry. If someone does a power number on me, I have this knee-jerk reaction to do a power number back . . . and win. But there was something about Adam that I liked.

"I didn't want to shove him away," Emily went on, "but I didn't want to go to bed with him just then. I wasn't feeling ready to sleep with him. I'd been through that with men I didn't really know very well, and it never worked. The relationship just felt too new."

In the discussion that followed we attempted to focus on Adam's feelings, rather than only on Emily's. We questioned why he was pushing, rather than asking or allowing Emily to offer him something. Why did he seem to feel that he wouldn't get anything he wanted unless he pushed and grabbed? Emily decided that the next time she and Adam were together she would address his feelings rather than respond to his actions by pushing him away. And she did.

"We got together for dinner and then went back to my place. And, just as I anticipated, he began pushing again. He kept grabbing at me and pressuring me . . . like a kid in high school. I said, 'Adam. Please stop pushing me. When you push like that I get angry. It's not that I'm trying to protect my virginity. I just don't feel ready yet. I like you. When we have sex I want it to be because of that. Not because you're pushing and grabbing at me. And let's face it, it's not going to make either of us feel good to be in bed because you pushed us there.'"

Adam was quite touched by the fact that Emily thought enough about him to be able to say she liked him even when he was pressuring her. They spent the rest of the evening talking. What was all the grabbing about? Adam, it turned out, isn't all that secure about his sexual attractiveness. He couldn't believe that he'd get to first base with Emily unless he really pressed for it. Emily, on the other hand, wanted the pleasure of giving to Adam, and by pressuring her he was making that impossible.

The night was a big success. Emily was thrilled by her newly discovered ability to talk to Adam in a genuinely intimate way. She said it felt as though a burden had been lifted. They continued to see each other and, of course, eventually added sex to their relationship. Regardless of where that relationship goes, it was a watershed for Emily.

"With Adam I was somehow able to let down my defenses. And I've had those defenses up for a long time. I've always thought that as soon as I sleep with a guy he loses interest. But with Adam that issue was different. The issue was that he didn't think he could get me without grabbing. And he didn't appreciate having things he got by grabbing."

The specifics of Emily's problem with Adam are less important here than the dynamic between them. Instead of dealing exclusively with her own anger, Emily forced herself to look at what Adam was communicating about himself. Once she recognized that he felt he couldn't get anything freely—without grabbing it—she began to feel some sympathy and warmth toward him. She saw his vulnerability instead of only seeing her own. That shift in thinking—from addressing one's own feelings to making room for another set of feelings—opens up the possibility for an intimate relationship. It's the same kind of thing Kate did when she accepted the fact that George had a booming laugh.

There's a normal wear and tear when you live with someone day in and day out. Intimacy is not, by any means, all rapture, sweetness, and delight. But it adds up to what life is all about. The normal wear and tear—the willingness to live with the little irritations—*is* intimacy. And our willingness to put up with another *real* person releases us from the enormous burden of seeking perfection in others and ourselves.

Love Vs. Intimacy

The issue for the women we have just described is, first, to recognize the difference between the kind of intimate relationships they can't live without and the kind of "loving unions" they can't live with; second, to recognize when they, or their partners, begin to slip from the former to the latter; and third, to set themselves back on the right course.

Learning to recognize the difference between "love" and "intimacy" is not difficult. It's an intellectual process, and intellectual insight is a valuable first step when one makes an effort to change old patterns of behavior. Slipping from the former to the latter is inevitable, however. It happens in the best of relationships. It doesn't mean a relationship can't work. It simply means it *needs* work. And the work it needs, although difficult and often frightening (as we'll see in the next chapter), is possible.

CHAPTER 10

Fear of Intimacy

Many career women, married as well as unmarried, find the prospect of an intimate relationship, as we defined it in Chapter 9, frightening. They don't come right out and say that intimacy scares them. Indeed, many of the women we interviewed don't even know that they're afraid. But the fear is evident in what they say and do about men and relationships.

Over the years, these women have constructed elaborate systems of defense that protect them both from their fear (indeed, from their feelings in general,) and consequently from intimacy as well. Women who say, for example, "There are no men out there," or who blame men in other ways for the fact that they are not in relationships (as we discussed in Chapter 4) are, for the most part, frightened of intimacy. They ward it off by thinking of "men" in general, rather than one specific man with a name and feelings of his own.

But saying "There are no men out there" is only one of many ways in which women avoid intimacy. The defense systems by which women guard against intimate relationships are myriad and highly individualized. We couldn't possibly presume to list them. We can, however, discuss those defenses that cropped up most frequently among the women we interviewed and suggest that the reader generalize from them to her own experience.

Autonomy Vs. Distance

Earlier, we defined intimacy as an egalitarian relationship between two autonomous people in which both focus on feelings more than on accomplishments. On an intellectual level most of the career women with whom we spoke found the notion of such a relationship exciting. On an emotional level, however, when it came down to the nitty-gritty of their lives, they found it frightening.

"I don't want to get involved in a relationship with a man who isn't very successful," said Laura K., a corporate lawyer, "because I don't want to risk being poor. I don't need a guy for that. I worked too hard to avoid it." But, we pointed out, you earn a great deal of money yourself. Your income wouldn't be any less if you married a man who wasn't in the same earning league. "You're right," she said. "I know that what you're saying is right. But it just isn't the way I feel. I can't help it. I don't feel safe being the primary breadwinner."

The fact is that Laura does feel safe being the primary breadwinner—*as long as she's the only breadwinner.* Her sense of herself as an independent, competent, autonomous person is very strong *as long as she's alone.* The presence of a man is tantamount to a threat. What is the threat about?

Laura is frightened of closeness. She wants to be in a relationship, but when she begins to consider an intimate connection with a man—a connection premised on the mutual acceptance of both strengths and vulnerabilities—she fears that she will have to surrender her autonomy. To wit, she doesn't fear losing her job until she is faced with the possibility of a relationship. The thought of being close to a man evokes fear in Laura.

She projects that fear onto the man. "He'll make me be dependent on him," she thinks. "He'll be threatened by me and want me to be deferential. He won't find me attractive if I'm really independent." But the fear Laura experiences, like most fears, comes from within herself. It is a projection of her inner conflict. Laura fears that if she is in a relationship *she* will reveal her desire to be taken care of. Indeed, she fears that her desire to be taken care of—a desire rooted firmly in her childhood AVBs—will override her desire to be an autonomous adult and come to rule her life.

Laura needn't deal with her fear of dependency when she is *not* in a relationship just as someone who fears the water needn't deal with that fear when they stay on high ground. Her childhood AVBs concerning male/female relationships simply aren't relevant when she isn't involved with a man. When she is, however, those old AVBs loom large, and she fears that she'll get mired.

Many women, like Laura, are frightened of their hidden dependency desires. It was this fear that Colette Dowling addressed in her book *The Cinderella Complex*. The very same women who are able to shape their own lives from nine to five—make important decisions, say "yes" to some things and "no" to others—feel that they will lose control when they're involved with a man. "He'll want me to be dependent," they fear. "I'll be dependent," they conclude.

This fear is not warranted. The autonomy Laura has developed has meaning in her life. It is real. It is a part of her identity. But it is not nearly as precarious as she fears. Indeed, the autonomy she has worked so hard for was not given to her by a man; and a man cannot take it away. The question is whether or not Laura will take it away from herself— whether or not Laura will feel obligated, once she's in a relationship, to lose herself to the man.

We don't think she will. It's entirely possible that Laura might slip, from time to time, into a more dependent role with a man than she finds comfortable. She might find herself acting "like my mother." She might find herself acting like the "good girl"—the deferential wife—prescribed by her childhood AVBs. But when Laura and women like her begin to feel uncomfortable because they've become too enmeshed with their husbands/lovers, they can stop and say, "Wait a minute. Something isn't quite right here. Let's go over what's been happening between us."

In fact, slipping in and out of dependency is part of being in a relationship. It is part of an intimate relationship (as we'll see in Chapter 11) for each partner to become too dependent, to recognize his/her discomfort, and to renegotiate. The dynamics of a relationship are never fixed in stone. When women own their own autonomy they can review what they do with it. Sometimes they may give some of it away. If they give away more than they're comfortable with, they can take some back. Men, to be sure, may want to take autonomy from women. They do, after all, have their own childhood AVBs to contend with. But men cannot steal away women's autonomy unless women cooperate. *And women need not cooperate!*

Most of the women we interviewed had a difficult time reconciling the existence of autonomy and intimacy within the same relationship. They could feel safe in relationships in which they were autonomous and distant—i.e., not emotionally vulnerable—or they could feel safe in lives with no relationships at all. But at best, intimacy for these women implied a merging; at worst, it implied a submerging.

Searching for a Mirror Image

Many women have attempted to avoid intimate relationships by seeking out their mirror image in a man, rather than looking for another person with whom to become involved. Laura, for example, wouldn't have to worry about being subsumed by a man if that man shared her every thought, feeling, and sensibility. Dory, the bond trader and theater devotee we discussed in Chapter 7, was a woman in search of a mirror image. She loved theater and couldn't imagine being involved with a man who didn't love it as much as she did. The fact that her boyfriend gave her two tickets to *Nicholas Nickelby* and expressed an appreciation of *her* love of theater was not enough for Dory. She wanted a duplicate of herself.

People have become so accustomed to hearing each other say they need a mate who shares their interests, that they've stopped asking why this particular kind of sharing has been elevated to the level of necessity. "He's not as smart as I am." "He doesn't have my sense of humor." "He's not as tall as I am." "He's not as verbal as I am." "He's not into the idea of therapy and I am." "He functions at a different pace than I do." "He doesn't have the same sense of esthetics as I do." "He's not athletic and I am."

You can only get that kind of duplication if you make a paper doll; at which point you are no longer talking about a real, live person. We said earlier that relationships involved sharing, which must involve both parties. The point of a genuinely intimate relationship is to open up and make room in your affections for another person who is willing to open up and make room for you.

Women who look to duplicate themselves need to stop and examine their motivations. Indeed, they have to ask themselves why their energies are more directed toward finding their mirror image than toward finding a tender, loving, entirely separate person. The fact is that searching for a mirror image is a pretty reliable way of avoiding a relationship entirely. Mirror images simply do not exist. They're not real. They can't be held, and they can't hold you. Real people, on the other hand, can do both.

"I was involved with a man about fifteen years ago whom I

cared for very much," said Julia S., a reporter with a large newspaper in Chicago. "We dated for about a year and one of our major activities was having these enormous fights over politics. He was a very conservative Republican. And I'm a liberal Democrat. At some point he asked me to marry him and I said no. How could I marry a Republican? It seemed impossible.

"Well," Julia continued, "I've dated lots of men since Roy. Some of them were very nice, others were less nice. But I've never met a man that I connected to in such a tender way as I did to him. I turned fifty-five last week and I've stopped thinking about ever marrying. But I haven't stopped thinking about Roy. The truth is that one of the things I missed when we split up were our fights. I think that even though we thoroughly disagreed with each other, we sparked each other. We each kept the other one thinking. They say hindsight is 20/20 vision, and as cliché as that might be, it's true. I really missed something special when I said 'no' to Roy. We had a special connection with each other that was more important than our political affiliations."

No Time for Intimacy

One of the ways women avoid their need for intimacy is to deny how lonely they are. They deny their loneliness by avoiding it; they avoid it by keeping busy. It's important here to distinguish between *saying* that you're lonely, and genuinely *experiencing* loneliness. Saying that you're lonely is an intellectual statement. It's an idea, and as such it has an abstract quality. "Of course I'm lonely," one woman said. "But what can I do? There's no point in dwelling on it."

The actual experience of loneliness, however, is a feeling. It's much more immediate, and it evokes an intense yearning to be with somebody. Indeed, that yearning is so intense that many women block it out. They may give it lip service, but they avoid the actual feeling by filling their lives with activities.

Ambitious, successful women are undoubtedly busy. Their work places enormous demands on their time. There is a distinction, however, with being busy and being afraid to not be busy. Consider Angela D. At forty, she is vice president in charge of personnel at a Fortune 500 company.

"My workdays are very long," Angela explained. "It's not unusual for me to get home at nine o'clock. And I do quite a bit of traveling—going to conferences and universities. I'd say that my work is the most consuming thing in my life. I also swim two evenings a week, and I have two subscriptions: one to the ballet and one to the Philharmonic. Those activities are very important to me. They're true relaxation. It's embarrassing, but I find myself booking dinner dates with friends months in advance. I just don't have any time."

Angela went on to say that she never really gave her hectic schedule much thought. "I always felt that my constant running was basic to my nature," she said. "I used to joke about not knowing where I'd fit a man in," she said, "but I never really focused on the whole thing until recently." Angela lives in a two-bedroom co-op on Central Park West in New York, which, until recently, she shared with her cat Contessa.

"I know that there's something very stupid about this intense attachment to an animal, but 'Tessa was very important to me. She was who I came home to. She'd meet me at the door and rub up against me to welcome me home. And in the morning she woke me up to get her breakfast. I mean, I had her for nearly eighteen years!" Angela reached into her bag for a tissue and laughed, even as she began to cry. "This is so stupid. I can't believe I'm still this upset about a *cat* for God's sake."

A few weeks earlier Angela's cat had begun to show signs of illness. She was very old and had lots of ailments that Angela knew about. But quite suddenly she seemed much worse. Angela stayed home from work and took the cat to her vet who suggested she be put to sleep. "I just couldn't handle it," Angela said. "So I brought her home and held her for a few days. I made broth for her and took her to another vet who said that she was old and riddled with tumors and that the kindest thing I could do was put her out of her misery. So with that kind of second opinion I didn't really have any choice. I put her to sleep."

When Angela came home that day without her cat she experienced her loneliness. Indeed, she experienced it for many days thereafter, and the experience of that loneliness was excruciatingly painful. "I just couldn't bear it," Angela explained. "I went back to work, and I tried to keep very busy, but the loneliness I felt when I lost Contessa just stayed and stayed. I thought for a while about getting another cat, and I probably will; but the truth is that I need more than a cat in my life. I need a relationship. And I know it now in a way I didn't know it before. I think I was shocked into that recognition."

That "recognition" is important to Angela and to other women who fill their lives with activity as a defense against loneliness. The painful experience of loneliness is a powerful motivation. In Angela's case, it led her to examine and, ultimately, to reevaluate her criteria for judging men.

Looking for a Mind Reader

Many of the women we interviewed avoided sharing their feelings in an egalitarian relationship by making men responsible for those feelings. For example, Edith F., a thirty-five-year-old woman who left a successful career as a publicist for law school, complained about her husband Bob's insensitivity. "He knew that I was absolutely crazed studying for the bar, and when I found out that I'd passed I called him immediately. You'd think he might have brought home flowers or something. But instead, he came home with some takeout Chinese food. I couldn't even look at him all night."

Why did Edith expect flowers? "It's the most natural thing in the world," she said. "Flowers are celebratory." Apparently, Edith and her husband have different ideas of what constitutes a celebration. She likes flowers and he likes hot and sour soup. It would be one thing if Edith were simply disappointed—everyone experiences disappointments in the course of a relationship—but Edith was furious, and felt unappreciated when her husband didn't celebrate in *her* style.

"Did you think to tell him you wanted flowers?" we asked. "Tell him to bring me flowers? Of course not," Edith responded. "If you have to ask for things like that they lose their meaning." The question is, what does Bob's bringing or not bringing flowers mean to Edith? In essence, she has equated his loving her—his appreciating her—with his bringing flowers; an equation that makes it difficult for Edith to ask for what she wants, and necessitates that Bob read her mind.

The truth is that bringing flowers does not reflect Bob's love or appreciation of Edith. Many men with less loving feelings toward Edith might bring her flowers every night. Bob doesn't think in terms of flowers. That is, at worst, a limitation of his. The issue for Edith is how she chooses to deal with that limitation. In a relationship in which she is autonomous, if she wants flowers she has two options. She can go out whenever she wants and buy herself flowers; or she can say to her husband, "When something special happens I'd like you to bring me flowers. Try to remember, and if you don't, I'll try to remind you."

Bob's response to Edith's direct statement about what she would like is a more significant barometer of his feelings for her than whether or not he can anticipate her wishes. He might say, "Gee. I never thought about bringing flowers. You know, in all of my memory my father never brought flowers to my mother. It doesn't come naturally to me but I'll try to remember." Or he might say, "I never liked the idea of bringing flowers to a woman because all of the phoniest guys I knew in college were always doing it." Or he might say, "When my mother was dying in the hospital, her room was filled with flowers. Ever since then I've had a bad association to cut flowers." Indeed, flowers might mean something entirely different to Bob than they do to Edith.

Edith finds the idea of asking for things frightening, because asking makes her vulnerable. It reveals that she has needs; and she doesn't want to feel needy. What if Bob says "no"? What if he gets angry? "What if he thinks I'm stupid for caring about whether or not I get flowers?"

Clearly, if Edith were to talk to Bob about her wish for flowers both she and Bob would stand the chance to learn something about each other. Such a conversation would, unquestionably, promote intimacy. Indeed, as we said earlier, the ability to reveal one's needs and vulnerability is the essence of an intimate relationship.

Many successful career women fear that if they allow themselves an intimate relationship they'll lose their autonomy. In order to protect themselves from losing that autonomy they avoid intimacy with a wide range of behavior. They rationalize why they can't have a man. They maintain emotional distance from the men they do meet. They cling to an image of themselves as being invulnerable—an image that men read as "unavailable." They search for men who are their own mirror images because they don't believe that a relationship can accommodate differences. Or they seek extensions of themselves by looking for men to anticipate their thoughts and wishes—men who can read their minds.

The fact is that there *is* a part of these women that comes from their childhood AVBs that says, "I need a man to take care of me." That part, however, is not their totality. Career women needn't feel so helpless in the face of their desire to be dependent. They can acknowledge their desire to be taken care of and acknowledge their autonomy as well. They are complex people with a wide range of feelings and they can find room for all of those feelings—even if some of them conflict. They can be sometimes dependent, and sometimes depended upon. And, as we'll see in Chapter 11, they can voice their dissatisfaction with the dynamics of their relationship *within the framework* of that relationship. Indeed, that sort of review, negotiation, and renegotiation is part of being in a relationship.

CHAPTER 11

Walking Through
an Intimate Relationship

The Process of Building Intimacy

All of the *clichés* about "falling in love" are, as we said earlier, significantly different from the realities of building an intimate relationship. An intimate relationship is not something that happens in a blinding instant: It really does require effort. An intimate relationship is an ongoing process. In fact, to some degree intimate relationships are never realized. In that respect, they're like 'justice,' an ideal we are always working toward but never fully achieve. The substance of an intimate relationship, therefore, is this process of working toward intimacy.

INITIAL ENCOUNTER

The first stage in building an intimate relationship with a man is, of course, the occasion when you first meet him. How you meet him—whether on a blind date, in college, at a party, or at the office—is much less important than what happens when you meet him. How do you feel at that first encounter? "Well," Alexis K. said when she thought back to her last blind date, "either something clicks or it doesn't. On my last blind date nothing clicked. I mean, it may have clicked for him—he was shocked when I didn't invite him into my apartment for coffee—but it didn't click for me."

Indeed, on an experiential level, that is precisely what happens on a first encounter. Something clicks, or it doesn't. But what triggers the "click"? Ideally, a first date is the time to determine whether or not you're interested in having a second date. Is this a man you'd be interested in getting to know?

This is also the time you begin to use your criteria for judging men. Many women (and men also) bring shopping lists with them on their first dates that hark back to their childhood AVBs. Alexis, a thirty-eight-year-old financial analyst, is one such woman.

"Some friends of mine set me up with Dana, a man they'd met a few summers ago at the tennis courts near their summer house. They thought he was nice, and they were right. He's a very nice guy—really sweet. We had a very pleasant time with each other. But nothing clicked. I mean, he just didn't seem like my type. He was built very weirdly . . . he had this very big head and a sort of sunken chest. And he was wearing navy blue polyester pants.

"My friends called the next day to see how it went and I told them that he was nice but no dice. When I mentioned the way he dressed they were surprised. They said that they'd only seen him wearing jeans or tennis shorts. I guess he thought he was getting dressed up for me or something. I don't know. I'd probably go out with him again if he called, but it doesn't have any future. And I think he realized that when I didn't invite him in."

When Alexis has a blind date her list of requirements includes such things as "well dressed" and "well built." When she meets a man who doesn't satisfy the requirements of that list, nothing "clicks."

The problem is (based on all we said earlier about external and internal criteria) there's nothing on Alexis's list that will help her find a man with whom she can share an intimate relationship. Polyester pants, sunken chests, or bulging biceps have nothing to do with intimacy. You cannot mine the inner recesses of someone's soul on a first date, but there is a great deal of important information you can pick up from conversation with a stranger, and if your list of criteria focuses on externals, chances are that you won't be able to focus on the things that matter.

Indeed, many women who rely on shopping lists of external criteria never get to the point of knowing anything important about the men they encounter. Carla, for example, is a thirty-eight-year-old woman who owns her own boutique. She told us about a party she'd been to recently to celebrate a friend's birthday. "There were lots of people there—about fifty—and I knew several of them. I got myself together for the party and, I must say, I looked pretty terrific. But the party was pretty much of a bust and I got home feeling depressed. While I was there I just talked to the people I knew. It's not that I was counting on meeting a man there, but it would have been nice. And the men there seemed like real losers."

How so? "Well, there was one guy there who was single, but he was shorter than I. And he spent the entire party with a pair of aviator sunglasses on top of his head. It was the most idiotic thing I'd ever seen. The party was on a Saturday night in the middle of January, and here he was with sunglasses on his head. And there was another guy there, who had a very irritating voice, who was wearing a pair of baggy jeans and a black turtleneck, with black socks and the kind of sandals people wore in the sixties. And about midway through the party he took off the sandals and spent the rest of the evening in his stockinged feet. I really can't stand that sort of thing. I mean it really disgusts me."

Carla didn't say one word to either of the two men she

described, and neither one of them made an effort to talk to her. It's no wonder. Her voice reflected such contempt when she described them that she must have conveyed her feelings, in one way or another, to them. She might have made a point of avoiding eye contact with them. Or she might have spent her time at the party sitting with her hands folded in front of her and an angry expression on her face. Regardless of how much effort she put into making herself attractive for the party—regardless of what she was wearing, how her hair looked, and how her body looked—there's nothing attractive about anger, contempt, or depression. Her outward appearance may have said, "Come here," but her inner emotions emanated a stronger message: "Stay away!"

"Well," Carla said, "that's fine with me because I had no interest whatsoever in having either of those men approach me. If what you're saying is true it just means that my inside was conveying the message I wanted it to convey." The question, of course, is how Carla could be so certain that she had no interest in either of those men. What did she know about the man with the glasses on his head? What did those glasses on top of his head reflect about anything that was happening inside of his head? Suppose, for example, that he had put the glasses on earlier when he drove to the party—it was a snowy day and the glare might have bothered his eyes—and then forgot that he had pushed them up on his head. Or suppose that he was balding and thought the glasses might in some way camouflage that. Or suppose he simply thought there was something neat or cool about wearing glasses on top of his head. Even if Carla felt otherwise, why did those glasses make him someone unworthy of a conversation? And why should the fact that he was short make him unworthy of a simple "Hello."

Carla might have had a better time at the party if she had gone with the idea of meeting and talking to people, instead of having gone with the idea of "finding someone." Either of the two men she described might have seen a good movie recently. Or read a good book. Or held an interesting job. Or been nice, and tender, and gentle, and warm. Carla didn't have to interact with them with the idea of marriage, or even dating. She might have simply had a pleasant conversation. But she couldn't allow herself that because her list got in the way. And she left the party feeling depressed and contemptuous.

What should be important to a mature person who wants an intimate relationship is the feeling she gets from her first meeting with a man. Rather than focusing on externals—like the fact that he wears a gold Rolex or drives a Mercedes, or that he went to the right college or has the right job—she should ask herself what her feelings are during the conversation. Does it feel good to talk with this person? Does talking with him make her feel uneasy or comfortable? The activity of a first date is, after all, conversation, and you can learn more about someone by paying attention to the dynamics of that conversation than you can from its specific content.

What can you expect to learn from the conversation of a first date? First of all, you can determine whether or not the man you're with is interested in you. Does he seem to be listening to what you say? And if he *is* listening, does he seem to understand you? Does he treat the things you say with respect or make fun of them? Does he make room for you to learn something about him? More important than the old shopping list of criteria on a blind date is the issue of whether or not you are with a man who will make room for you, respect your autonomy, treat you tenderly, and let you into his life.

This is how Alexis described her conversation with Dana, her blind date. "He was actually very easy to talk to," she said. "He started off by asking me how I felt about blind dates. He said that he'd always felt very nervous about them but when push came to shove they were the easiest way to meet women. He hated the idea of going to singles' bars. I agreed with him. I hate that whole meat-rack experience. I must admit that I felt very comfortable with him at that point because he had picked up on something that we could really share—our discomfort with the situation we both found ourselves in.

"Then we talked a bit about being shy. He's very shy and I said that I thought of myself as being shy but people who know me don't think I am. Most people think of me as being very outgoing but sometimes I feel that's just a front. I feel that if I act very outgoing I'll *be* very outgoing. He said something very sweet about how hard it is for one person to know what was going on inside someone else."

Alexis was right. Dana did, indeed, say a very sweet thing. He might have started laughing out loud when she said she was shy. Alexis does not come across as being the least bit shy. He might have said something like, "Right. You and Charo and Joan Rivers are a bouquet of shrinking violets." Instead, he respected what Alexis had to say about herself, heard it, and thought about it.

"We talked a little about what we were like as kids," Alexis recounted, "He didn't have the greatest childhood. He was an only child and his parents were quite old when he was born and they were very nervous all the time. They're both dead now. Then he started talking about opera and the truth is that I can't stand opera. So I let him talk and waited and waited for him to stop, but he just kept going. That's when I began losing interest."

Why hadn't Alexis said that she didn't like opera? "I didn't want to hurt his feelings," she explained. The fact is that when Alexis began losing interest in the conversation about opera she also began losing interest in Dana. It's likely that Dana tuned in on Alexis's loss of interest and experienced that rejection. Had Alexis been less interested in pleasing Dana by posing as someone other than herself—i.e., a woman who is interested in opera—she might have been able to let him know that she liked him even though she didn't like opera. And Dana would have come out of the evening feeling more connected to the real Alexis. If Alexis had said, "I never really liked opera," they might have talked about what they liked or didn't like about it. In tuning out Alexis was really closing a door without exploring it adequately.

BEGINNING A RELATIONSHIP

If Alexis hadn't shut the door on Dana, she could have moved on to the next stage of building an intimate relationship: dating. The point of dating is to confirm or disprove your first impressions. If, for example, Alexis thought Dana was a sweet, sensitive, interesting guy, and began dating him, she'd begin to see whether that impression of him was correct or he had just acted sweet and sensitive on that first date.

When two people are dating they should be trying out their relationships. Are they comfortable with each other? Why? Why not? Does he give you something? Does he offer you warmth, friendliness, fun, helpfulness? Will you let him? Do you give him something? Will he let you? Is he a nice person? Does he meet the criteria we discussed earlier for an intimate partner.

Getting to know a man during this stage of a relationship is not a matter of his making a detailed and comprehensive statement about himself so much as it is a process of discovery. You can't sit down with someone on a first date, or a second, or a third, and proceed to educate them about you. You can't say, "Let me tell you about myself. I'm phobic about heights because I had a traumatic experience on a flight of steps when I was a child. I have a pretty short fuse but get over my anger just as quickly. I can't tolerate procrastination," and so on. People need to learn about each other experientially, and the time to do that is while they're dating.

Let's take a look at some examples of how they might go about doing that.

Joan and Thomas

A thirty-six-year-old woman named Joan had dated a man named Thomas a few times. She liked him, but she was also troubled by some things about him. She thought he often seemed distracted . . . as though his thoughts were somewhere else. And she said that he wasn't polished. At best, he was a diamond in the rough. At worst he was just plain rude and inconsiderate. For example? "The last time we went out," Joan began, "we had dinner in a restaurant near where we both work. The dinner went very nicely. In some respects, we were just beginning to get comfortable with each other. But then, when we were leaving, he walked out of the restaurant ahead of me and just let the door slam in my face."

What did that mean to Joan? "I was mortified," she said quickly. "I felt he was either a total boor, or he just didn't care about me. In fact, I'm not sure I'd even want to see him again, except I have this nagging feeling that there's something really very nice about him."

We asked Joan to tell us about their evening in detail, to reconstruct their conversation. She began with some background. She and Thomas had seen each other three times before this date. She lives in Tribeca and Thomas lives on the Upper West Side of Manhattan, and they hadn't yet been to each other's apartments. They'd met in the course of their work—he was an architect and she was in real-estate management—and their dates, so far, had all been on weekday nights after work. This date, which took place on a Friday night, was the first time they'd seen each other on a weekend.

"Let's see," Joan thought back to the dinner. "At dinner we started talking about work and books and movies. And he told me how touched he was by a movie he'd just seen in which he identified with a very isolated little boy. I asked what was the little boy like, and Thomas said, 'he was very sweet and gentle, and no one ever listened to him.'

"And then," Joan continued, "he talked a little bit about money. He said he was feeling particularly broke these days because he had just taken a share in a summerhouse in the Hamptons. I told him that I was trying to figure out what to do with my summer and he suggested that I come out and take a look at his house. He said there were still some shares open and I might want to buy into it. I felt a little nervous at the suggestion because who knows if we'll still be seeing each other in three months, so I declined. I tried to be tactful. I said something about not wanting to be in a group situation and thinking about possibly taking a trip instead.

"And then the check came. I offered to split it with him because it ended up being more than we thought it would be, but he said no. So he paid the bill, we put on our coats, and we started to leave. He was several paces ahead of me and he just opened the door up and let it slam right in my face."

Having reconstructed her evening with Thomas, it seemed clear that he didn't slam the door in Joan's face because he didn't care for her. In fact, it seems entirely possible that the door was slammed in her face because he did care for her.

He began the dinner by telling her that he identified with the little boy in the movie he'd just seen. He said, essentially, that he often feels like a child who no one listens to. Then he told her, by asking her to take a share in his summerhouse, that he liked her very much and envisioned their involvement continuing into the future. Joan, of course, had every right to accept or reject the invitation, but the fact is that in rejecting it, she left him feeling somewhat rejected and vulnerable. At which point the bill came and, being more than he had anticipated, added to his vulnerability.

Thomas, clearly, was very interested in Joan. Most probably, he spent some part of the evening anticipating what would happen after dinner. How could he get an invitation to Tribeca? How could he get her to come to his place? This had never really been an issue before because they always had work the next morning, but the next day was Saturday, and Thomas was acutely aware of the difference that meant when he asked Joan out. The problem is that, whether due to temperament or to limited experience with women, he isn't very aggressive sexually. And he has a particularly hard time with his desire for Joan in the wake of her rejection of his proposal to her on sharing a summerhouse with him. "If she were interested in spending the night with me," he'd probably thought, "she wouldn't have been so quick to turn down a share in my summerhouse." Could Thomas risk being shot down twice in one evening?

Those were the dynamics. Thomas was neither ill intentioned nor ill spirited. His behavior didn't stem from a rejection of Joan. Rather, it came from a desire for her. In fact, when Joan opened the door for herself, he turned to her and said, "Oh. I'm sorry. I wasn't thinking." To which Joan replied, "That's all right," while fuming and thinking to herself, "You obviously aren't thinking of me." Thomas probably wasn't thinking about holding open the door for Joan because the good-night scene was approaching and, in light of their evening together, he was preoccupied with how it might go.

What could Joan have done? She had a number of options, several of which would have put an end to the relationship. For example, she might have exploded on the spot. "You're one of the rudest, most thoughtless men I've ever met," she might have said, and taken a taxi to Tribeca. Or she might have held her anger in but given Thomas a passive message: been cold, withdrawn, or sulky. "He's not the only one who can be self-involved," she might have said to herself. Or she might have simply turned herself off with a thought like "The last thing I need in my life is someone like him. I deserve a man who's thoughtful enough to hold open a door."

If, however, Joan were interested in promoting the relationship she could have glossed over what she perceived as his rudeness, and gone home to think about it. She might have asked herself how he had experienced the evening. If she had come up with the kind of assessment we just came up with, she might have continued to date him; and she would have done so with a better understanding of his nature. Thomas, she would have realized, is not all that sure of himself, and when he gets anxious, he gets caught up in his own thoughts and desires.

Another possibility for Joan, if she had allowed herself to get involved with Thomas, would have been for her to say, "You seem preoccupied. What's on your mind?" This response would have helped take the guesswork out of their relationship. Joan cannot control the degree to which Thomas is able to open up, but she can create an environment in which he can feel safe with his feelings. Ideally, Thomas might have responded by saying, "I'm not looking forward to saying good night." But if he could have responded to her more openly, he might have sensed her warmth and friendliness.

The point of dating is, as we said, to get to know someone . . . not to fall in love. While dating you have an opportunity to see if the qualities you like in a man are consistently present. This assessment and reassessment needs to be both intellectual and emotional. When you respond emotionally from your childhood AVBs, your reactions need to be reassessed, despite the fact that that process can be difficult. It isn't impossible. Such an evaluation prevents you from closing doors prematurely.

Of course, it's important to understand that human beings have frailties and vulnerabilities. And if we want an intimate relationship, we must accept human frailty and make room for it in our lives. Thomas, for example, might have had an awful day at work. He might have spent the entire evening preoccupied with a deal that fell through; or thinking about the fact that his mother was ill; or that his child was having problems in school. These are all possibilities that need to be considered. And then you have to ask, "Is he a decent, loving person who wants to make room for me in his life?"

The case of Phyllis and Jeff illustrates another impasse that can happen in the early stages of a relationship.

Phyllis and Jeff

Phyllis, a forty-year-old television newswriter, lives in downtown Chicago with her five-year-old daughter. Not too long ago she began dating Hugh, a man from nearby Evanston. After spending a lovely spring Sunday with him she began to think about selling her apartment in the city and moving to a house in Evanston.

When she mentioned the idea to Hugh, he said, "Why don't you and Dory come out here for the day next Saturday and I'll give you both a personal guided tour? If you want we can even go to some brokers and talk about what's available. And I'll make dinner for us all." Phyllis accepted his offer and was feeling very excited about the plan. But as Friday rolled around she began to think differently. Dory was very happy and doing well in her school. They had lots of friends where they were. The move began to feel more and more like a bigger upheaval than she thought she wanted.

Friday night she called up Hugh and canceled. "I told him that I had changed my mind about moving to Evanston so we wouldn't be coming out on Saturday. He sounded kind of disappointed for a minute but then said that he'd be in conferences until Wednesday but would speak with me when he was finished. Meanwhile," Phyllis said, "Wednesday came and went and Hugh didn't call. Now I feel like he isn't going to call me and I'm really pretty upset about it. I really like him. He's a special person. I'm not sure I realized how much I liked him until a few days ago when I met another guy at a Sierra Club meeting. This guy was all right. We went out to dinner together after a hike and I ended up going to bed with him. The next morning all I could think about was how much more special Hugh was."

Did Hugh know that Phyllis thought he was something special? Did he know that she liked him? "I don't know," Phyllis replied. "I mean, he might have felt rejected when I said I wasn't going to come out to Evanston."

Why not call him up and make certain that he knows you like him? "Oh no," Phyllis said quickly. "I couldn't do that. I mean, suppose he really isn't interested in me. After all, he said he would call and then he didn't. If I call him I might be making him feel uncomfortable. That wouldn't be fair. I couldn't do that." So Phyllis and Hugh's dating came to an early standstill, despite the fact that Phyllis recognized Hugh as being a special sort of man.

The fact is that when Hugh offered to spend the day with Phyllis and her daughter—to show them around the neighborhood and make dinner—real estate was probably very low on his list of priorities. He was making a date. He was planning a day for them to all spend together. And when Phyllis canceled that date because she lost interest in moving, she was, essentially, telling Hugh that she was only interested in him as a real-estate contact. From Hugh's perspective it was quite clear: If Phyllis was interested in him, regardless of whether or not she planned to move, she would have kept her date. She could have called him and said, "Look. I've decided not to move, but I'd still like to see you. Why don't we make some other plans for Saturday?" Clearly Hugh didn't feel comfortable enough with Phyllis to let her know that he was hurt. Instead, he withdrew by parrying with a quick "I'm busy too," and then made a retreat.

Phyllis's fear of calling Hugh is a projection. She said that she didn't want to call him because it would have made *him* feel uncomfortable when, in fact, she didn't want to call him because it would have made *her* feel uncomfortable. She didn't want to put herself in the position of revealing her vulnerability. Indeed, men talk all the time about how vulnerable they feel when they have to call women who might or might not be interested in them. "What if I let him know that I like him and want to see him, but he doesn't want to see me?" she asked. "What if?" we replied. What are the possibilities?

Let's look first at what actually happened. Phyllis decided not to call Hugh, and chances are, he will never call her. She isn't certain whether his not calling has to do with his mistaken belief that she isn't interested in him or with a genuine lack of interest on his part. The relationship is over.

Suppose Phyllis's worst fantasy was realized. Imagine that she called Hugh and let him know, either directly or indirectly, that she liked him and wanted to see him again and he let her know, either directly or indirectly, that he wasn't interested. Phyllis would be in pretty much the same situation she's in now. The relationship would be over. There would, however, be one significant difference. She wouldn't have to entertain the possibility that a relationship she cared about had ended because of fouled-up communications.

Another possibility is that Phyllis could call Hugh and let him know that she likes him. People like hearing that they are liked. She could invite him to dinner. Or she could say that the last time they talked, when she canceled the day they had planned together, she had been so anxious about the idea of moving that she was afraid she hadn't been very sensitive to him. And that she was sorry about that.

If Phyllis decided to pursue either of the latter two paths, she would, indeed, be pursuing an intimate relationship: an egalitarian relationship that addresses feelings rather than appearances. But the truth is that those kinds of relationships frighten Phyllis. She doesn't want to express her real feelings because doing so makes her feel vulnerable. She'd rather be involved with a controlling, traditionally macho man who plods along without intruding on her inner feelings. Such were the men with whom Phyllis had been involved. Although she felt victimized by them, she also felt safe. The

men who were insensitive to her never insisted on knowing
what was going on inside her. Of course relationships like
these—which were rooted in Phyllis's childhood AVBs—
never worked out in the long run because they lacked genuine intimacy.

Susan and Vince

Susan, a thirty-one-year-old designer, met Vince, a stockbroker, at a tennis match. They spent a good deal of the
evening together and, before he left, Vince asked for Susan's
number. He called her a few days later to see if she wanted to
get together over a cup of coffee. When she said yes, he
suggested that he might come over to her place. She agreed,
but hung up feeling angry. She believes that when a man
suggests coming into her apartment it's because he's only
interested in sex. But she didn't say, "No, I'd rather meet you
at a nice little coffee shop around the corner." Instead, she
said, "OK." In fact, she went several steps beyond a simple
OK.

Susan prepared extravagantly for Vince's visit. She bought
French-roasted coffee beans, several expensive cheeses, and
good English crackers. But her anger escalated while she
shopped. By the time Vince rang the bell she was fuming
inside. "He came in and made himself very much at home,"
she explained. "We talked while he ate and drank, and the
more he ate and drank the angrier I became."

Susan is a very successful woman, but she sets up situations
with men in which she feels completely powerless and
manipulated, and, ultimately, resentful. If Susan had suggested that she and Vince meet at a coffee shop, she might
have learned something about him by the way he treated her
suggestion. For example, she might have said, "I'm really not
all that comfortable having men I don't know very well up at
my place. How about meeting somewhere?" If Vince had
made fun of those feelings or disregarded them, she would

have had reason for not trusting him with her feelings and breaking off the date. But if he had treated them with respect, Susan might have learned something important about him.

This sort of learning is what this early stage of an intimate relationship is all about. How are your needs treated when you express them? Is he interested in you because he met you at the match and you're a new face? Or does he continue to be interested in you when you express emotions and stop talking about surface things? And what turns you on or off about him? Does he let you into his life? What does he let you learn about him?

Susan's evening with Vince turned out to be very upsetting for her. Susan had sacrificed her needs before Vince had arrived at her house, and she was angry with him about that before they had even gotten together. As Susan's evening with Vince progressed the dynamic became pronounced, and Susan's anger more palpable.

"We were both sitting on my couch when he made his move," Susan said. "We fooled around on the couch for a while and I was worried that it might get messed up. But if I'd told him *that* he'd have thought I was crazy, so instead I suggested that we go into my bedroom. But before we went in I told him that I didn't want to make love," Susan added emphatically.

What happened? "As soon as we got in there he began undressing me. Shortly after the sex he left and I felt just awful. I felt that he'd taken advantage of me," Susan concluded, "and I certainly don't intend to see him again."

Vince, obviously, didn't buy Susan's statement that she didn't want to make love. After all, when he called he suggested that they get together for some coffee. When he arrived at her apartment he found a seduction scene: an elaborate spread, including linen cocktail napkins. From his perspective it seemed that she was very eager to entertain him. And when she suggested that they go into the bedroom, what was he supposed to think? She may have said that she didn't want to make love, but actions speak louder than words. And from Vince's experience, women often seem to feel obligated to resist a bit before they have sex with a man for the first time. That resistance is as much a part of their childhood AVBs as Vince's ability to ignore it is a part of his.

Based on Susan's first encounter with Vince, she drew certain conclusions which were rooted in her childhood AVBs. Vince was a successful stockbroker and a go-getter. He asked for her number up front, and followed up shortly thereafter with a phone call. Translation: Vince was a "good catch." Based on Susan's childhood AVBs he was "marriage material."

Susan went about "hooking" this "good catch" with a method clearly prescribed in her childhood AVBs. She set out to please him. The problem is that when Susan defined Vince as a good catch she automatically became a woman who *needed* a good catch. Her identity as an independent, valuable, separate person was swallowed up by her childhood AVBs. She felt helpless and fearful. And she felt angry at Vince for evoking those feelings. Her anger was, of course, a projection.

WORKING OUT A RELATIONSHIP

If any of the women we've been discussing had gotten beyond the stage of dating, they'd have found themselves at a point where they would have had to get down to the nitty-gritty and work out a relationship. An important part of this process is negotiation. Each person must be willing to relinquish control, to make his/her needs clear, and to make concessions. The concessions for men and women are different. They each have to let go of their childhood attitudes, values, and behavior and focus more realistically on their adult aspirations. For women that means letting go of their fantasy of being cared for by a powerful man, and accepting the responsibility of being an equal partner in a relationship. Ultimately, the kind of autonomy we're talking about means accepting responsibility for oneself, rather than accepting responsibility for one's partner.

It is, as we'll see, a big responsibility, particularly when it comes to making your needs known. In hierarchical relationships (or what most of us grew up thinking of as love), a great emphasis was placed on two people's ability to anticipate each other's desires, each within the context of traditional gender roles. Women were supposed to somehow know what men wanted for dinner. And men were supposed to know what to buy their wives for Christmas. The healthy manifestation of all this "anticipating" required sensitivity; the neurotic manifestation, as we'll see, involved the expectation that one's partner could read minds.

Terry and Peter

Terry, a very successful real-estate broker, had been married to Peter, a partner in a brokerage firm, for nine years when she turned forty. "I had strong feelings about my fortieth birthday," she explained, "and I wanted to have a big bash to celebrate it. I kept dropping little hints to Peter about how important this birthday was to me, and I was hoping he'd come through with a party for me. But my birthday came and went, and there was no party. I felt neglected, really hurt. Peter bought me a lovely necklace, and we went out to dinner, but I really wanted a party and he was oblivious to that."

We asked Terry if she had told Peter that she wanted a party. "No," she replied. "If you have to ask for that kind of thing it loses its meaning." Terry wants Peter to be a mind reader. But she's taken that expectation one step further. If he doesn't know what she wants, it's because he's not listening. And if he's not listening, it's because he doesn't love her.

There are, of course, all sorts of problems with Terry's

expectations. To begin with, Terry has lost sight of the fact that a party might mean something very different to her than it does to her husband. In fact, as we talked, it became clear that Peter hates parties. He doesn't much like going to other people's parties and the idea of having one thrown in his honor—where he'd be the center of attention—is horrifying. So it's understandable that he wouldn't dream of giving a party for his wife.

Secondly, Peter might have been preoccupied with things that seemed more important to him than Terry's birthday. He might have been having problems at work. He has his own neuroses, his own struggles and conflicts. The fact that a birthday party is important to Terry doesn't mean that it has to be important to Peter. And, if the two of them are involved in a genuinely intimate relationship, the fact that a party isn't important to Peter doesn't mean that he doesn't care about Terry.

We asked Terry if she had thought about making herself a party. And she was shocked. "How could I do that?" she asked. Terry, who is capable of organizing the closing on a three-million-dollar house, is perfectly capable of planning a party. But she was shocked at the idea of taking care of her own emotional needs more than at the logistics involved for a party.

The more we talked about the idea of Terry giving her own party, the more intrigued she became with the idea. For there's something liberating about recognizing one's ability to make oneself happy. "Actually," she concluded, "that's a wonderful idea. Peter will be delighted that I'm doing it for myself. He'll even be thrilled to pick up the tab. He loves giving me things but worries about whether or not I will like them. This way I can just tell him that what I want for my birthday is a fabulous party, and all he'll have to do is arrive in a tux. He'll be relieved, and I'll have exactly the kind of party I want."

This resolution is significant. When a partner in a relationship thinks productively about how she can take care of her needs without hurting her partner, she's less likely to end up feeling angry and disappointed. Terry feels much more in control of her life when she doesn't rely on Peter to read her mind. And the more in control of her life she feels, the more tenderness she'll feel for Peter. This is the hallmark of intimacy. Peter and Terry don't need to prove anything to each other. They need to trust their commitment to each other.

Carl and Lenore

Carl and Lenore have been married for twenty years and have two daughters. For the first eight years of their marriage they tried to have children. "It looked as though we weren't going to have kids," Lenore said. "I had a very hard time getting pregnant, and the two occasions I did conceive I lost the baby in the first few months. Carl didn't really say very much about it. At one point after I had a miscarriage he tried to comfort me by saying that it wasn't the most important thing in the world to have kids. We both had work that we loved. Carl makes a great deal of money, and I do all right. He started talking about travel and all sorts of other things we could do if we didn't have kids.

"But I was feeling more and more that I wanted to have a child. In fact, I wanted to have at least two children. I really wanted a family. And in the months that followed my miscarriage I realized what I wanted to do. I wanted to adopt. The problem was that I didn't think Carl wanted to adopt. I figured that if he wanted to adopt a child he'd have said something to me. And he hadn't."

Lenore, who loved Carl very much, was operating by a double standard. She assumed that Carl would express his desire to adopt while, at the very same time, she was withholding her desire to adopt a child from him. Why should Lenore think that Carl would be any more likely to initiate discussion about adoption than she was? Indeed, Carl might have been every bit as eager to get the procedure going as Lenore was, and every bit as frightened. "If she wanted to adopt," Carl might have thought, "she'd have said something. I guess she doesn't want to."

Why was Lenore afraid to express her desire? Because according to her childhood AVBs it is her husband's job to know what she wants and get it for her. She, the "helpless" partner, should be "taken care of." By contrast, an autonomous, egalitarian relationship provides room for both partners to express wishes and desires . . . even if they can't be realized.

Finally, Lenore mustered her courage and told Carl that she wanted to adopt. "I do too," he told her. "When should we start?" "I said we might as well start immediately," Lenore explained, "and we did. I picked up the phone, called an agency, and we began pursuing a family together. Until I came right out and said what I wanted, I think both of us wanted the other one to take care of this big hole in our lives. We both wanted a mommy to come and make it all better. And it wasn't going to happen that way."

Both Lenore and Carl acted from the system of their childhood AVBs. Their energies went into attempting to read each other's minds rather than into communicating their own feelings.

Gloria and Jerry

Gloria didn't begin her career in advertising until ten years ago when her children were in high school. Despite her late start, however, she's become extremely successful. She's an account executive with a large New York agency. One of the most difficult issues of her marriage—which has become particularly sensitive since her career success—is that she often feels that her husband attempts to control her. "All day long," she explains, "I manage to handle enormous responsibility—I make decisions concerning how hundreds of thousands of dollars should be spent—and when I come home Jerry treats me as though I were a child. He's always steamrolling me into decisions with which I'm not all that comfortable. At work, I don't doubt my competence, but at home, after twenty-five years of marriage, he wants me to check everything out with him."

At work Gloria operates by her adult aspirations, but when her childhood AVBs take hold, she begins to feel dependent and inadequate. However, rather than look at her problem in terms of what's happening inside of her, Gloria blames it on Jerry. "He steamrolls me," she says, rather than, "I feel steamrolled." The significance of that difference becomes apparent when Gloria describes the last fight she and Jerry had.

"A few weeks ago," she begins, "we were driving out to our beach house on a Friday afternoon. I had picked Jerry up at his office, so I was driving. There's a point on the highway where you have to merge left, and you can do it from either of two lanes. Jerry always does it from one lane because he feels it's safer, and I've always done it his way without even thinking about it. On this particular Friday I thought, as I approached that point, that it might be better to do it from the middle lane. So I stayed where I was but drove very slowly and carefully. All of the sudden, out of nowhere, a car shot in front of me and I had to swerve in order to avoid a collision. It was really pretty scary.

"Jerry, of course, began yelling and screaming about why hadn't I gotten over into the other lane the way I should have. He kept ranting about how he always gets way over to the left expressly to avoid this sort of thing, and how there are all sorts of maniacs on the road, and we could have gotten killed. What was the matter with me? Didn't I have any sense? I really felt like I was this five-year-old being scolded by her daddy. It was mortifying. And, of course, I went on about how I was an adult and could use my own judgment. I kept asserting myself verbally, but I felt just dreadful inside."

Although Gloria asserted herself *verbally*, emotionally she accepted Jerry's judgments; not only of her driving but of her worth.

"We had an awful weekend. I just couldn't even look at him without feeling rage until Sunday night when I cooled down a little. The truth is that my anger is still there, weeks later. I feel like I have to walk on eggs around him so that I don't make any mistakes because he'll seize the opportunity to demean me. I mean, I think Jerry loves me. We've been married for a long time, and in many respects we have a good marriage. He's very proud of my work, for example, and he's always very accommodating about my schedule. But this is a real problem, and I'm getting more and more angry about it."

The problem, as Gloria identifies it, is that Jerry demeans her. The real problem, however, is that Gloria accepts Jerry's judgment of her. She feels demeaned because when she comes home from the office—where she genuinely feels independent and confident—she begins to rely on Jerry for her identity. When Jerry tells her she has "no sense," she believes him. If, on the other hand, Gloria felt confident and independent she would have been able to recognize that when Jerry screamed in the car, he was really out of control and panicking. After he'd calmed down she might have been able to say, "The guy in that car was an absolute lunatic. That must have really frightened you. It did me too."

If Gloria had been able to address Jerry's reaction in terms of his panic she would also have appreciated the strength of her own reaction. Gloria was frightened too, but she didn't lose control.

Barbara and Frank

Barbara and Frank have lived together for two years. Frank, a radiologist, is a very laid-back person. He's on staff at a medium-size Connecticut hospital, likes his work, and has no interest in pursuing a private practice, despite the fact that he could easily double his income if he did. Barbara, an MBA, works in the telecommunications industry and earns $85,000—good money in that field, but not nearly as much as she could earn in other areas of business. Unlike Frank, Barbara is ambitious.

"I enjoy my work," she explains, "but I realized that my current income was probably as high as I could go, and that bothered me. I began to think about other directions I might go into with my MBA, and the truth is that I'm pretty aggressive. If I can make $150,000 I want to do it. I thought about that for a while and decided to pursue some other paths, and I ended up with an offer from a brokerage house with a starting salary that's more than I'm making now, and the sky's the limit. And I began to panic."

What was Barbara's panic about? "I felt that I wanted to take the job but at the same time I was frightened by it. When it was offered to me, they made such a big deal about the amount of work involved. They said that I should expect to work twelve- or fourteen-hour days. There's a lot of pressure. I'd lose a lot of vacation time that I've accumulated. I find myself asking whether I'm willing to take all of those negatives along with the positives. The night I was offered the job Frank and I had dinner with some friends. I told them about the offer and they both had the same reaction. 'What do you need it for? You make a reasonable living. Why do you want to trade in a very comfortable situation for a pressured one?' And Frank pretty much agreed with them. By the time we got home that night I'd pretty much decided to turn down the job offer. I was worried that Frank didn't want me to take it; that he'd feel turned off to me if I took it; that it was sort of unfeminine or something. And I was feeling pretty depressed.

"When Frank and I got into bed I asked him if I should take the job. And he said 'Look. I can't tell you that. You know me. I'm a low-keyed person. I wouldn't want it. But it might be right for you. You like to work under pressure. You're going to have to think about it and decide what's best for you."

Barbara went on to say that Frank's attempt to answer her question simply fired her panic. "I think I really wanted him to tell me what to do. It would have been much easier if he'd just taken the whole thing out of my hands. It's hard to be an adult and have an adult relationship. That night I really would have preferred to have an old-fashioned relationship where Frank could be a scapegoat. In fact, he wanted to make love, but I just couldn't think of it. I was too angry about the fact that he wouldn't take charge of my life."

Barbara made the effort to examine her anger. She recognized, in doing so, that it was difficult to be in an autonomous, egalitarian relationship, but she also recognized it's value. Ultimately, she valued her relationship with Frank enough to take responsibility for herself.

MAKING A COMMITMENT

The idea of commitment is critical to the success of an intimate relationship, and commitment hinges on whether or not the partners trust each other. Long-term relationships can't always be wonderful. There are good times, and there are bad times. There are limitations to what intimacy can provide, and in a committed relationship there is room for those limitations. One doesn't *always* feel loving. One cannot *always* "be there" for one's partner. No one is *always* able to keep a check on his/her self-involvement. Life often intrudes on intimacy. Everyone, man and woman, sometimes acts in ways that run counter to the best interests of a relationship. But if both partners value the relationship and want it to endure, then they have the foundation for commitment.

When there is a genuine commitment, both partners find that they can relax, and that their relationship is, in the truest sense, a haven. You don't always have to be on your best behavior. A full life touches the whole range of our emotions, and a truly intimate relationship takes it all in. You can be in a lousy mood without worrying that your partner is going to pack up and move out. You can express anger, grief, and greed, and you can listen to your partner express those same things without fear that your relationship will break up. Of course, letting your hair down shouldn't transform you into a full-scale witch. The base of intimacy remains tenderness and caring. And commitment stems from that base.

Consider the situation of Richard and Mary. They'd been married for four years when Mary became pregnant. Mary, at thirty-one, was a story editor for a major film studio in Los Angeles. Richard, a few years older, was a screenwriter who, at the time they decided to have a child, was 90 percent certain of an important contract. Unfortunately, the contract didn't pan out, and over the course of Mary's pregnancy Richard's career did a nosedive.

"By the time I began my last trimester," Mary explained, "Richard was terribly, terribly depressed. I'd get home from work every day and he'd be sleeping. When he was awake he just talked on and on about how angry he was at everyone: at his agent for not pushing through the deal; at the producer for dumping it; at all of his friends in the industry for 'disappearing' when he needed them. He had no interest in the pregnancy at all.

"I remember when the baby began moving I once put his hand on my stomach to feel it, and he was incredibly impatient. After about thirty seconds he pulled his hand away and snapped something about not having all night to wait around for a fetus to move. And he went into the living room. Basically, I was alone during the pregnancy.

"The final blow came when I was about to go into my ninth month," Mary recalled. "Richard went out for a run and nearly collapsed on the living room floor when he returned. He started to cry and finally said that he wanted to die. He began talking about how he might kill himself. Should he jump out a window . . . or take pills?

"Until that point I did everything I could to be supportive of him. I kept trying to look for solutions. I felt like I really wanted to help him. But when he said that he was going to kill himself—and leave me with this baby in my stomach—I started pounding away at him. A few months earlier, when it was evident that Richard just wasn't going to be there for me during this critical time in my life, I had gone into therapy so I could manage to create some kind of support system for myself. But it was one thing to *not* be supported by your husband, and it was quite another to have him threaten to abandon you. I remember lying on the floor punching him again and again and screaming, 'How dare you? . . . how dare you?'

"That was such a painful time for us. It made *Scenes from a Marriage* look like a sitcom. When can it possibly be more important for a man to be there for his wife than during pregnancy? And mine wasn't. There's just no way of getting around that fact. He wasn't there.

"But somehow we survived. Time has a way of passing. Lila was born. Richard managed, somehow, to be a terrific Lamaze partner. And shortly after Lila was born he got a job. Little by little he got himself together . . . back to the way he was when we fell in love. I told him the night of the big scene that I just couldn't handle his depression anymore, and that if he valued our relationship he'd have to get help. And he did. He began therapy and really started dealing with his depression. In some ways he's a very different person now."

Richard and Mary had a deep and abiding commitment to each other and to making their marriage work. The commitment motivated them to look beyond the events—and even beyond their individual needs—to each other's feelings. Mary trusted that once Richard understood the serious consequences of his behavior—and once he understood that she had reached her limit—he would do his best to change it. Despite his pain, he forced himself to listen to his wife.

"The other night," Mary continued, "we were talking

about that whole painful period of our life and I felt very strong. . . . I felt that somehow our relationship was very strong and rooted and that we'd been through a lot of life together. Richard said that he still feels depressed sometimes, but that he understands that he's responsible for taking care of his depression. He knows that he can't make it my responsibility and I know that no matter how much I love him I can't assume that responsibility." Their relationship is emotionally egalitarian and they are both autonomous within it.

"When Richard feels that he's in charge of his own depression he feels a little bit more in control of himself and, I guess, a little less depressed," Mary concluded. "I guess we've sort of come to the conclusion that marriage isn't the same as being in confession all the time. We're two very separate people and we have to take care of ourselves. It's just nice that we've got each other around when we come out of our crises."

"Being there" is what commitment is about. Partners in an intimate relationship cannot necessarily meet all of each other's needs all the time, but they can hope for some success in meeting those needs. Anything more than that is unrealistic. Indeed, anything more than that interferes with intimacy. Someone who is always thinking about meeting the needs of another person eventually comes to feel overburdened, whether he or she is aware of it or not. People cannot simultaneously be in touch with their partner's every need and pursue an ambitious career as well. They can only do the best they can, let each other know that they care, and that they will stand by them. That is the nature of the commitment that Mary and Richard worked out.

REWORKING

Relationships are as alive as the people in them. As people change over the course of time, the relationships they are in must change in order to accommodate them. Indeed, the true test of a committed relationship is how well it endures changes in the lives of its participants. If the relationship is founded on the criteria for intimacy that we discussed earlier, chances are that it's going to have more room for growth than a relationship that was entered into on the basis of the partners' external attributes. If a man married a woman because she had large breasts, for example, both he and his wife are less likely to survive the trauma of a mastectomy with their relationship intact. If a woman married a man because he had a glamorous career, she's less likely to be a comfort to him if he loses his job.

Relationships don't only need to be reworked as a result of crises, however. We've all read about the "empty-nest syndrome"—the problems women have when their children leave home and they are suddenly left without the stuff that filled their days: the meals for four, the car pools, the laundry, etc. Men undergo similar stress when they retire and, for the first time in forty years, are faced with the prospect of spending long days in their homes with their wives. Essentially, couples who are fortunate enough to grow old together find that they are continuously dealing with new terms in their relationships.

"When Jim retired," his wife explained, "he just assumed that we'd do everything the way we always had. That I'd have breakfast ready for him in the morning and the house clean, and the laundry done. Well, I wanted to retire also. The way he had things set up there would never be a time for me to retire. So, after a pretty difficult time, we managed to divide things up fairly. Jim does all the vacuuming and dishwashing. It was a big thing for him, because he'd never lifted a hand in the house. I didn't mind it all that much when he was working outside the home, but now that he's not, it's only fair that he do something. And he agreed . . . reluctantly."

As men begin to accept the fact that women are involved

in important careers and are accepting a shared financial responsibility for their families, they will be more likely to reevaluate their own career goals. And when men begin to do that, the dynamics of their relationships will no doubt change.

Joan C. is a thirty-seven-year-old lawyer who's been married ten years. "When we were first married," she began, "Serge had been out of architecture school for about a year and was making something like $15,000 at a small firm. He hated what he was doing—all the drudge work of the firm— but he believed that if he stuck with it he'd eventually get to do some of the exciting stuff. I was a second-year associate with a big New York law firm and was making about $40,000. Not too long after our wedding Serge's father approached him about going into the family business.

"Serge's father and uncle manufacture children's clothing and they have a very successful business. They came to Serge with a proposal because someone had offered to take over their company for many millions of dollars but they wanted to keep it a family business. The deal was that Serge and his cousin would ultimately inherit the whole thing, and that they'd start at a salary of $50,000 a year. Well, Serge had absolutely no interest in children's clothing, but how could he turn it down?

"So for the last ten years he's been working in this business. We have lots of money, and we have a very expansive lifestyle. The only problem is that Serge hates going to work every morning. I mean, he really hates it, and he's started having problems with his father as well. It's all coming to a head now. Basically, Serge wants to quit. He says that he really wants to be an architect. That's what his training was for, and that's what he loves.

"Well, I'm trying to be very supportive," Joan said, "but the truth is that I'm terrified. I mean, I make a good living, but it's one thing to make a living when you know your husband is there to bring in the big bucks. Serge's salary as a beginning architect is going to be about a tenth of what we're accustomed to. Our expenses are huge. We've got two kids in private school, a co-op to maintain, a garage. All of those responsibilities are suddenly going to be on my shoulders and even though I make a good deal of money, I don't know if I'm up to it."

Joan and Serge began to study their life-style and make cuts. They rented out their country house for the summer season. They had their two daughters tested for gifted programs in the public schools and have begun to think about pulling them out of private school. Ultimately, Joan felt that she had no choice but to make room for Serge to leave his father's business. "But it's going to be very difficult," she concluded. "Serge is a very easygoing guy and I've always admired that quality in him. I don't think I'm going to admire it quite so much when I'm working my tail off to pay our monthly maintenance bill. It's going to be a very rough road ahead."

The best thing Serge and Joan can do is attempt to keep their lines of communication open. Their adjustment is not dissimilar to the kind of adjustment many men had to make when their wives left home for the workplace. Joan, over the next five years, will be confronting, on a daily basis, her childhood AVBs. And so will Serge. He was not raised to be subsidized by a woman, any more than Joan was raised to support a family. No doubt, the kind of stretching they both need to do to accommodate this change will strengthen their marriage. But it's difficult to keep a long-range perspective in the heat of battle.

Throughout this book we have addressed ourselves to the fact that in many important ways women today are different than women of a generation ago. In the course of our research we interviewed three hundred ambitious, successful career women. They said, with rare exception, that they believed they had a different sense of themselves than women before them had. That they wanted *different* things in their lives. That they wanted, and expected, and fully intended to get *more* from life than their mothers had.

Much of what these women spoke about initially wanting was work-related. They wanted meaningful work. They wanted success. They did not want to be dependent on men; rather they wanted to be able to rely on their own resources. And those resources were most impressive. The women were bright, hardworking, dedicated, creative. And they were willing to make personal sacrifices to get what they wanted.

As these women came closer to reaching their initial goals in the work world—after years of professional training or low-level apprenticelike positions—they began to question whether or not they really did have more from life than their mothers had. They began to wonder if the cost of their careers had to be lives without intimacy. Married women began to fear that in some oblique way their careers were interfering with their marriages. Single women began to wonder if they ever would find suitable men with whom to share their lives. They all expressed a deep yearning for intimacy and tenderness; for partners in their high-pressured lives who could hold them and comfort them, and whom they could hold and comfort as well. They expressed what we described earlier as the desire for an "adult family." Why had fulfillment in their personal lives eluded them? How might they go about finding it?

In the course of our interviews we discovered that the very same women who genuinely prided themselves on a new, independent identity were also troubled by what they considered to be the implications of that identity. Women who were autonomous all day long still wanted to feel cared for when they came home from the office. On an emotional level, feeling "cared for" was awfully close to being "taken care of" and being "taken care of" was uncomfortably close to the kind of relationships they were trying to escape. They learned, as children, that women were supposed to be deferential to men, but when they went out into the work world they boldly, and courageously, rejected that aspect of their earliest education. They were, however, less able to make a clean break with their pasts in their relationships with men than they were in the work world. These relationships were fraught with ambivalence.

The women we interviewed are struggling to come to terms with who they've become. It is, as we've seen, a difficult struggle that involves integrating the past with the present. Successful women need to examine their childhood AVBs, along with the AVBs of the workplace, to see which will be of help and which will be a hindrance in their personal lives.

We have every reason to believe that women as motivated and talented as the ones we have encountered in the course of writing this book will be able to find personal fulfillment. Women learned, early in the Women's Movement, that they can no longer afford to feel helpless. They are learning now that they cannot afford to deny their tenderness.